✫✫✫✫✫✫✫✫✫✫✫✫✫✫✫✫

BASEBALL
SUPERSTARS

Mike Piazza

✫✫✫✫✫✫✫✫✫✫✫✫✫✫✫✫

✦✦✦✦✦✦✦✦✦✦✦✦✦✦✦✦✦

Hank Aaron

Ty Cobb

Lou Gehrig

Derek Jeter

Randy Johnson

Mike Piazza

Kirby Puckett

Jackie Robinson

Ichiro Suzuki

Bernie Williams

✦✦✦✦✦✦✦✦✦✦✦✦✦✦✦✦✦

✳✳✳✳✳✳✳✳✳✳✳✳✳✳✳✳✳✳

BASEBALL SUPERSTARS

Mike Piazza

Nick Friedman

CHELSEA HOUSE
PUBLISHERS
An imprint of Infobase Publishing

✳✳✳✳✳✳✳✳✳✳✳✳✳✳✳✳✳✳

For Caroline. What a year.

MIKE PIAZZA

Copyright © 2007 by Infobase Publishing

Chelsea House
An imprint of Infobase Publishing
132 West 31st Street
New York NY 10001

Library of Congress Cataloging-in-Publication Data
Friedman, Nick.
 Mike Piazza / Nick Friedman.
   p. cm. — (Baseball superstars)
 Includes bibliographical references and index.
 ISBN-13: 978-0-7910-9493-8 (hardcover)
 ISBN-10: 0-7910-9493-6 (hardcover)
 1. Piazza, Mike, 1968– 2. Baseball players—United States—Biography. 3. Los Angeles Dodgers (Baseball team). I. Title. II. Series.

 GV865.P52F75 2007
 796.357092—dc22   2007006212

Series design by Erik Lindstrom
Cover design by Ben Peterson

Printed in the United States of America

Bang FOF 10 9 8 7 6 5 4 3 2 1

This book is printed on acid-free paper.

All links and Web addresses were checked and verified to be correct at the time of publication. Because of the dynamic nature of the Web, some addresses and links may have changed since publication and may no longer be valid.

☆ ☆ ☆ ☆ ☆ ☆ ☆ ☆ ☆ ☆ ☆ ☆ ☆ ☆ ☆ ☆ ☆ ☆

CONTENTS

1

Greatest
Hitting Catcher
of All Time

Mike Piazza had one thing on his mind when he stepped up to the plate for the first time in the New York Mets' game against the San Francisco Giants. It was May 5, 2004, and the Mets' slugger desperately wanted to hit a home run.

Hitting homers was as natural as breathing air to Piazza. In 11 years in the big leagues as a catcher, he had smashed 351 round-trippers of every kind: line-drive rockets, towering moon shots, bottom-of-the-ninth blasts, crushing grand slams. Piazza knew, however, that the next ball he sent screaming over the fence would be something special, something for the ages. The next home run would guarantee him a place in baseball history.

Trouble was, Piazza had been trying too hard to hit homers lately. A good hitter needs to be relaxed in the batter's box and focus on making solid contact with the ball. If a home run comes, it is a bonus. Piazza had been "pressing at the plate" as major leaguers say, and it showed. After belting three home runs in his first two games of the season, he had gone 16 games before clearing the fence again. Then came another dry spell of six games.

Would tonight's game against the Giants at Shea Stadium in New York be number seven?

It would not take long to find out. Mets manager Art Howe had written Piazza's name into the third spot of the batting order, the place typically reserved for a team's best all-around hitter. The "three-hole" hitter swings a bat as skillfully as an artist wields a paintbrush. He usually collects plenty of hits for a high batting average. Yet he also has the power to launch the ball deep into the outfield and even into the seats for a homer. His main job is to drive in the first two batters in the lineup should they get on base. Because he was batting third, Piazza was getting his first crack at making baseball history in the bottom of the first inning.

Tonight, however, the first two Mets batters made outs, leaving the bases empty when No. 31 stepped into the batter's box. Piazza, a right-handed batter, dug his feet into the dirt and took some practice swings with his 32-ounce bat, the same model he had used since his days in the minor leagues. Out on the mound, San Francisco pitcher Jerome Williams, just 22 years old and in his second big-league season, took a deep breath and got ready to go head to head with one of baseball's most feared power hitters.

Williams wound up and threw his first pitch. It sailed outside the strike zone, and Piazza wisely let it go by for ball one. The umpire signaled ball two when the right-hander's next pitch missed the plate again. Was the showdown making Williams nervous?

Two pitches later, the count was three balls and one strike, giving Piazza an advantage. Like a hungry wolf about to devour a big, fat lamb chop, Piazza knew that Williams would have

★ ★ ★ ★ ★ ☆

HOW DOES A BATTING ORDER WORK?

A baseball manager is free to arrange his team's batting order any way he likes. Through the years, though, a common wisdom has developed about where to place certain types of hitters in the order to produce the most runs. Here is the thinking: The job of the leadoff hitter is to get to first base any way he can—through a walk, a single, a bunt, even getting hit by a pitch—and then move into scoring position. For that reason, he is usually one of the fastest runners on the team. The number-two batter is also fast and should be able to make good contact with the ball to help advance the leadoff batter. The third batter may be the best all-around hitter on the team and will drive in a run or get on base himself. That brings up the cleanup hitter. Usually the most powerful batter, he is there to clean the bases of runners—think of what happens when a batter smashes a grand slam.

The fifth hitter also packs power, can drive in runs, and may have another job: to "protect" the cleanup hitter through his presence as a strong hitter. An opposing pitcher who fears the cleanup hitter and wants to walk him on purpose will think twice about that strategy if he knows the fifth hitter can drive him in. The sixth batter is a power hitter as well and collects RBIs, and the seventh and eighth batters are generally not good hitters. They still need to be able to reach base, however.

Finally, the ninth place in the order is typically reserved for the pitcher in the National League and, therefore, is the weakest of all at the plate. In the American League, however, a designated hitter bats in place of the pitcher (in another part of the order). That opens the ninth spot to a more skilled hitter. Some managers like this player to have skills like the leadoff hitter to ignite the team if he happens to come up as the first batter in later innings.

to throw his next pitch for a strike or risk walking him with ball four.

Williams gripped the ball inside his glove and then reared back and delivered a fastball toward the plate. Piazza feasted on fastballs. This one came in low, but Piazza reached down and swatted it, putting all 215 pounds (97.5 kilograms) of his muscled body into the swing. Whack! The crack of the bat sent the ball arcing high into the nighttime air. No one was going to catch this baby. It flew way over the fence in right-center field and bounced off the lower part of the scoreboard, 405 feet (123 meters) away from home plate. That ball was out of here!

Piazza had done it. He had blasted his 352nd career homer, breaking the all-time record for home runs by a major-league catcher. His name would be written alongside the immortals of the game forever. With a happy smile on his face, Piazza trotted around the bases as the dramatic theme music from the movie *Chariots of Fire* echoed over the stadium's speakers. When he reached home plate, Piazza's teammates swallowed him up in a sea of high fives, chest bumps, and helmet taps. Meanwhile, Shea Stadium's 19,974 fans stood up and roared their approval. Piazza ducked into the Mets dugout, but a few moments later, the crowd was still going wild. Piazza bounced back up and tipped his cap in thanks. The fans could not get enough of him. It was like a curtain call on the Broadway stage after an amazing performance by an actor.

After the game (which the Mets won, 8-2), Piazza felt relieved. With the pressure to hit his landmark homer finally off his back, the newly crowned King of Catchers told a reporter for the *New York Times,* "I'm really excited and really proud. I'm blessed. I've lived a dream."

Piazza's words were right on target. For those who knew his story and how he beat the odds to reach the majors, his accomplishment was indeed a dream—an almost impossible dream.

At Shea Stadium, Mike Piazza hit his 352nd career home run as a catcher in the first inning of a game between the New York Mets and the San Francisco Giants on May 5, 2004. With the round-tripper, Piazza passed Carlton Fisk as the all-time career home-run leader among catchers.

LONG ROAD TO THE TOP

Major League Baseball is filled with legendary home-run hitters. Babe Ruth, Hank Aaron, and Willie Mays are three of the greatest of all time. Each is enshrined in the National Baseball Hall of Fame in Cooperstown, New York. In today's game, superstars Manny Ramírez, Ken Griffey, Jr., and Alex Rodriguez are making their marks with awesome displays of power that will surely land them in the Hall of Fame one day, too. All six of those players have hit more career home runs than Mike Piazza. But none of them succeeded in the way Piazza did.

Few people thought Piazza had the all-around ability to make it to the big leagues. Growing up in Phoenixville, Pennsylvania, Piazza was an excellent hitter. When he was a senior at Phoenixville Area High School, his batting average was an astounding .442. He also belted 11 home runs. But Piazza had two glaring weaknesses on the diamond: He was a slow runner, and his fielding was poor (Piazza played first base at the time). As a result, no major-league teams were interested in the star from Phoenixville High.

Piazza went on to play college baseball. After hitting .364 in his sophomore season, the Los Angeles Dodgers chose Piazza in the 1988 draft of amateur ballplayers. Usually, players with the most major-league potential are chosen in the first two rounds of the draft. Other solid players may be taken in the third or fourth round. Los Angeles selected Piazza in the sixty-second round—after 1,389 players had already been taken. That is like turning a bag of potato chips upside down and dumping out the last salty crumbs.

Los Angeles sent Piazza to its lowest minor-league team for rookies, in 1989. The Dodgers had asked Piazza to switch positions from first base to catcher. Though catcher is one of the most demanding jobs in baseball, Piazza agreed. He figured the move would give him a better chance of making it to the majors, where hard-hitting "backstops" are a rare breed. Over the next four years in the minors, Piazza dedicated himself

Mike Piazza, playing for the Mets, tagged out Houston's Moisés Alou at home plate to end the ninth inning of a 2001 game in Houston. The Los Angeles Dodgers drafted Piazza way down in the sixty-second round of the 1988 amateur draft. Piazza switched from first base to catcher, one of the most demanding positions in baseball, in the hope of improving his chances to make it to the major leagues.

to mastering the skills behind the plate: giving signals to the pitcher, blocking bad pitches in the dirt, snapping off quick throws to second base to nail runners trying to steal.

Late in the 1992 season, the Dodgers brought Piazza up from the minors to give him a taste of the big-league game. The following year, Piazza's first full season in the majors, he gave the Dodgers a taste of *his* game—and the greatness to come. He hit 35 home runs, setting a big-league record for a rookie catcher. He also threw out 58 runners trying to steal, the most of any catcher that season. At season's end, Piazza was rewarded with the National League's Rookie of the Year trophy.

Now playing for his fifth team, the Oakland A's, the 12-time All-Star still thrills fans with his long-ball show while he adds polish to his Hall of Fame credentials. Piazza has won a record 10 Silver Slugger awards, an honor given to the best hitter at each position. His .362 batting average in 1997 was the highest by a catcher going all the way back to 1936, and it remains so to this day. In 2000, he drove in at least one run in 15 straight games, tying the longest RBI streak in major-league history. He swatted his 400th career homer in early 2006.

As a kid, Piazza adored everything about baseball and dreamed of playing in the pros. He practiced his batting stroke over and over, first in his family's basement and later in a backyard batting cage built by his dad. Given a rare opportunity to prove his worth in the minors, Piazza drove himself tirelessly to learn the position that would give him his best shot of making it to "The Show," as the big leagues are often called. When he arrived, Piazza set a new standard of hitting excellence for all major-league catchers to come.

Growing Up in Pennsylvania

Ask any boy what he wants to be when he grows up, and chances are, he will give you two or three answers: "I want to be a bus driver, like my dad," he might say. Or, "I want to test new video games." But you can bet two weeks' allowance that one of the answers will include a job in pro sports. "I want to play in the NBA." "I'd like to be the quarterback for the Pittsburgh Steelers." "I'm going to pitch for the New York Yankees and hit in the three hole after Derek Jeter and win Game 7 of the World Series at Yankee Stadium."

Who can blame a kid for wanting to play in the pros one day? Let's face it, sports stars rule. They are millionaires who drive fancy cars and have the coolest toys. They appear on television and sign autographs. Perhaps best of all, they play a game and get paid for it. That's not a job—that's pure fun.

the New York Yankees' home-run king and arguably the greatest baseball player of all time.

Mike's fascination with the sport was bred into him by his father. Mr. Piazza was a baseball nut raised in Norristown, across the street from a homegrown star named Tommy Lasorda. Although Lasorda was six years older, the two boys were friends. Blessed with serious talent as a left-handed pitcher, Lasorda played in the minor leagues in the late 1940s and early 1950s. He was called up to the big leagues by the Brooklyn Dodgers in 1954, but he just did not have the stuff to get major-league hitters out. He pitched only 26 games from 1954 to 1956 with the Dodgers and later the Kansas City A's, and he finished his career with a record of no wins and four losses. Lasorda, though, went on to greatness years later as the manager of the Los Angeles Dodgers. In 21 seasons in charge of the Dodger dugout, Lasorda led Los Angeles to eight division titles and two World Series championships (1981, 1988).

The year Mike turned eight, 1976, also happened to be when Lasorda became manager of the Dodgers. You have to know that Mr. Piazza was bursting every time his old Norristown buddy and the Dodgers appeared on television. Imagine the excitement, not to mention the mixed feelings that were stirred up inside Mike's dad, whenever the hometown Phillies played the Dodgers. Which team should he root for?

If you could take a trip back in time to the Piazza home on a Saturday morning in 1976, you would find Mike camped in front of the TV watching his favorite cartoons. Sticking around into the afternoon, you might catch a Phillies game with him on the radio. The Phils were Mike's favorite team. And what a team they were. In the 1976 season, Philadelphia won 101 games, its best regular-season record ever. They were led by left-handed strikeout ace Steve Carlton, who won 20 games that season, the mark of excellence for a major-league pitcher.

You would have to cheer for the Phils with Mike in the room, of course, but you had better go quiet whenever third

Tommy Lasorda was a pitcher in the 1950s with the Brooklyn Dodgers. He had much more success decades later as the manager of the Los Angeles Dodgers. Mike Piazza's father, Vincent, Sr., grew up across the street from Lasorda in Norristown, Pennsylvania. Their friendship would have a major influence on Mike Piazza's career.

baseman Mike Schmidt stepped up to the plate. Schmidt was young Mike Piazza's idol. It's no wonder. With a unique combination of power and fielding excellence, Schmidt was one of the best third basemen of all time. In 1976, No. 20 won the National League home-run title with 38 blasts, including four in one game against the Chicago Cubs. Schmidt played 18 seasons in the majors, slugging 548 home runs and winning three National League Most Valuable Player awards (1980, 1981, 1986). He retired after the 1989 season and was elected into the Baseball Hall of Fame five years later.

After the Phils game was over, you would grab a bat and head down to the Piazzas' basement, where it was time for some serious baseball work. Baseball? In the basement? That's right. Taking his son's passion for the game to heart, Mr. Piazza had propped an old mattress up against the wall so that Mike could practice hitting baseballs into it without the risk of breaking anything. Sometimes Mike hit the ball off a batting tee, and sometimes his dad would pitch to him. Crack-Thump! Crack-Thump! Crack-Thump! The rhythm of Mike's bat driving the ball into the frumpy mattress became a familiar sound throughout the Piazza house.

On Sundays, you would find the Piazzas at church. Growing up Catholic, Mike and his family attended services every week. "Religion, our faith, has always been a big part of our family," Veronica Piazza told the *Pottstown Mercury* newspaper in July 2004.

At age nine, Mike joined his first youth-league baseball team, the A's. His coach was a man named Abdul Ford-Bey, a legend in Phoenixville for his volunteer work with boys and girls in baseball, softball, and basketball. Ford-Bey taught Mike and his teammates the fundamentals of the game. The next year, Mike moved on to a team called the Cardinals. His new coach put him on the field as a catcher. Mike did not like the position. Like many kids first learning the game, he

One of Mike Piazza's childhood idols was Mike Schmidt, the third baseman for the Philadelphia Phillies. Schmidt hit 548 home runs during his 18-year baseball career in the 1970s and 1980s.

wanted to be a pitcher, the one player on the field in control of the game.

When Mike was 11, Mr. Piazza had a wild idea one day. One way that major leaguers improve their hitting skills is by practicing their strokes inside a batting cage with a pitching machine tossing ball after ball toward the plate. Mr. Piazza thought: Why not give Mike the same opportunity to improve his hitting skills—at home? So at a point when most fathers and sons were building go-carts together, Mike's dad got some lumber, and some netting, and made Mike his own batting cage in the family's backyard. Then Mr. Piazza took his plan one giant step further: He bought a real pitching machine and installed it inside the batting cage.

Mike was in heaven. The cage became his hangout for the next nine years. "I was out there every day," Piazza told *Sports Illustrated* magazine in 1993. "I would come home from school, get a snack, watch cartoons, and then hit." Mike smacked about 300 balls a day, no matter the weather—rain or shine, sleet or snow. In the winter, he would shovel snowdrifts out of the cage, heat the baseballs on the stove, and wrap pipe insulation around the bat handle so his hands would not sting when he made contact with the ball in the freezing cold.

Did all that practice pay off? You better believe it. "The more I hit, the better I did in Little League," Piazza told an interviewer in 2003. "By the time I was 13, I'd made the all-star team."

Eventually, Mr. Piazza made the cage more comfortable for Mike by adding a roof on top and enclosing the sides with wood paneling. He also put in a heater. The batting cage, though, was no thing of beauty by any stretch of the imagination. In fact, one day, some Phoenixville government officials visited the Piazza home to investigate the curious structure. As stated in the *Sports Illustrated* interview, when the officials asked Mr. Piazza what it was, he told them, "It's my son's ticket to the major leagues."

ONE TOUGH SPORTS PARENT

If it seems weird for a father to build his son a professional batting cage in the backyard and spend money on a real pitching machine, you are right. Most fathers do not do those things. But almost from the start of Mike's interest in baseball, Mr. Piazza was as obsessed with Mike's love of the game as Mike. Maybe even more so.

Vince Piazza was a man who drove himself hard in all that he did. Born poor, he dropped out of high school at age 16 to get a job and help support his parents. Mr. Piazza, though, was smart and aggressive. He was not going to let his lack of formal education get in his way of achieving the American Dream. He saved money as if it were going out of style. After buying a used-car dealership, he began to invest money in real estate and other interests. Around the time Mike was 13, his investments began to pay off and he starting earning big bucks. He bought more car dealerships. He also opened a computer services company. In time, he became a multimillionaire.

As the cash rolled in, Mr. Piazza invested more money— and time—into Mike's baseball talent. According to a 1994 interview in the *Los Angeles Times Magazine*, Mr. Piazza "decided that his son, like it or not, was 'gonna play baseball'" as a professional.

Why did Mr. Piazza focus on Mike and not his other sons? Here's how he answered in the same interview: "When Vince, Jr., and Mike were kids, I looked at them both and asked myself, 'Which one has the best chance of playing pro baseball?' Mike was younger, 11, but bigger. I chose Mike. I pushed and pushed that kid."

Today, this kind of sports parent is all too familiar. He's the father who likes to tell a coach how to run the team. The dad who buys his son all the top-of-the-line equipment before the old gear even gets dirty, demands special treatment from coaches for his son, enrolls his boy in training clinics year-round, and yells at the umpire if he disagrees with his calls.

Worst of all, he drives his own kid to succeed and criticizes him if he does not perform up to his expectations.

Mike loved his dad, and he appreciated his support. After all, Mike sought the same goal as his dad—to become a major leaguer. Years later, Mike realized that his father had at times pushed him too hard, too often. He would be labeled "spoiled" by others who doubted his talent, which hurt Piazza deeply. But when he was 11, 12, 13 years old, Mike followed his dad's wishes.

In the years to come, Mr. Piazza would use his influence and money to give Mike a series of golden opportunities to sharpen his game that would make any young baseball player green with envy. Mike, to his credit, would seize each one of those opportunities and use it to the best of his ability. One such opportunity included receiving batting tips at age 16 from one of the finest pure hitters the sport has ever known. It would be a moment Mike would never forget.

High School
and Beyond

Kids dream big. And playing pro sports is one of the biggest dreams they can have. In truth, though, the odds of making it to the pros are thinner than the last few hairs on a bald man's head. According to one study, only 1 out of every 736 high school players in football, basketball, or baseball has the perfect combination of skill, drive, and luck needed to reach the top level of his sport. In baseball, about 120,000 players each year are the right age for the major-league draft, but only about 1,200 are actually good enough to be drafted. To think about it a different way, major-league teams select just 1 kid out of the starting lineups of every 133 eligible baseball teams in the world each year.

That does not mean that a boy should give up on his dream of making it to the pros. It just means that it is wise to have plenty of other interests in life—interests that can inspire other big dreams. You never know: A hobby like taking pictures with the family's digital camera might lead to a career as a sports photographer.

WORKING NEXT TO HIS HERO

Mike Piazza's father may have known about the overwhelming odds stacked against his son ever making it to the pros—or of being drafted. Or maybe he did not. Chances are, even if he did know, he would not have cared. His goal was to give Mike every advantage he could to improve his shot at reaching the majors. One way he planned to do this was by asking for help from his old friend from Norristown, Tommy Lasorda.

In the years after Lasorda's promotion to Dodgers manager, the former childhood neighbors had grown closer. Vince Piazza had given Lasorda some smart investment advice and provided business opportunities that had earned money for both men. Lasorda was grateful to Mike's father and was eager to repay him by lending a hand with his boy from time to time.

One of Lasorda's first acts of gratitude occurred when Mike was 13. One day that year, Mr. Piazza arrived home from work and told Mike that the Dodgers were coming to town to play the Phillies. That was not such big news, since Los Angeles played in Philadelphia six times a season. The next piece of news, however, was big: Mr. Piazza had made an arrangement with Lasorda for Mike to be the Dodgers' batboy—not just for the next game but for every game the Dodgers played in Philadelphia.

Mike was thrilled. For years, he had watched his favorite team, the Phillies, and his idol, Mike Schmidt, on television and in person from the stands at Veterans Stadium in Philadelphia. Now, he would get to see Schmidt up close at work and maybe pick up some tricks of the trade along the way. Mike wasted little time in taking advantage of the golden opportunity given to him. Once on the job, the kid in the Dodgers uniform began to study the acclaimed Phillies third baseman as if he were the subject of a college course.

Known for his quiet focus and controlled emotions on the field, Schmidt took his work seriously. He did enjoy playing the game, but he preferred to keep his feelings to himself and not get too excited over a homer or too down after making an out. Mike noticed the way that Schmidt bounded confidently up the dugout steps and into the on-deck circle, the way the muscles in his powerful forearms would bulge as he swung the bat back and forth to loosen up. The way Schmidt dug into the batter's box with a sharp confidence that sent a menacing message to the pitcher: "You're mine." Years later, Piazza admitted that he patterned his own brand of baseball directly after Schmidt's. "I really admired the way Schmidt carried himself," Piazza told a reporter from *New York* magazine in 2000. "He was always very stoic, very serious. I like to have fun, but for some reason, if I do show emotion on the field, it's impromptu, it's not a lot of fist-pumping. I like to run my home runs out and walk back to the dugout."

In July 1996, Piazza's connection to Schmidt came full circle at Veterans Stadium. Piazza was then in his fourth full season with the Dodgers and was the starting catcher for the National League in that season's All-Star Game, played in the Phillies' home park. One of Piazza's duties that evening included catching a ceremonial first pitch thrown out by one of five retired Phillies being honored by Major League Baseball. Which Phillie threw his pitch to Piazza? Mike Schmidt, of course. Perhaps inspired by the joy of "playing catch" with his boyhood hero, Piazza went on to have a spectacular night. He hit a home run and a double to help give the National League a 6-0 win over the American League, and he earned the game's Most Valuable Player award. Afterward, Piazza was glowing: "For something like this to happen in Philadelphia is just unbelievable," he told MLB.com.

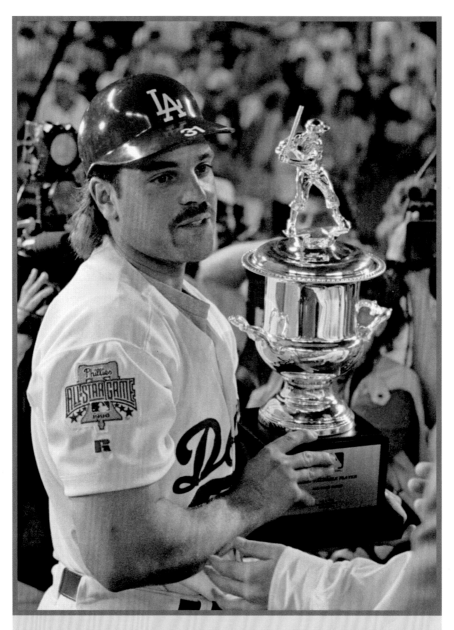

Mike Piazza won the Most Valuable Player award at the 1996 All-Star Game, which was played in Philadelphia. "For something like this to happen in Philadelphia is just unbelievable," Piazza said. Another highlight of that game was catching a ceremonial first pitch thrown by his idol, Mike Schmidt.

Mike served as batboy for the Dodgers in Philadelphia for the next several years while also playing youth league baseball. At home, he bashed pitch after pitch in the batting cage. His dream of reaching the majors fueled his ceaseless drive for improvement.

HEAVY METAL STUDENT

By now a 15-year-old sophomore at Phoenixville Area High School, Mike was known by his fellow students as the baseball nut with the home batting cage but also as a bit of a loner off the field. Although he had his solid core of friends in high school, Mike was not exactly Mr. Social. There simply was not much room in his life for anything other than baseball. "There was a time in high school when I started hanging out with friends and became socially active. And that's healthy to be socially interactive, but for me, once I saw that I wasn't missing out on a lot, I became more dedicated to what I wanted to do," Piazza said in the 2006 *Stack* magazine interview.

If you were to drop by the Piazza household when Mike was a young teenager, you would still hear the sounds of the Phillies game on his radio. Once the announcers reported the final out, Mike might snap off the game and pop a cassette into a tape player or drop a record onto a turntable. Then your ears would get a workout—a sonic workout.

As a teenager, Mike developed a passion for heavy metal music. The loud, aggressive, and often-angry rock music of the 1980s just seemed to hit the right note with the somewhat shy guy. He loved the roaring sounds of the power guitars, the crashing drums, and the screaming vocals of bands like Black Sabbath, AC/DC, and Metallica. With the volume cranked up, a hit song like AC/DC's "Back in Black," with its dark lyrics about an outlaw escaping from the hangman's noose, might shake Mike's room like a thundering volcano. The music became a kind of escape for the adolescent athlete from the pressures of baseball and his father. Inside his room, he could let the sounds wash over him and carry him to a place where no one judged his performance.

Devoted followers of heavy metal are known as "metalheads." Mike described himself at the time as a "metalhead-jock"—a guy who was into the music and who also played sports. The kids around school had no trouble figuring out Mike's musical tastes from the way he dressed. He typically wore jeans and boots and a black T-shirt with the name of a metal band written across the front. He had piles and piles of the shirts, bought as souvenirs at the "hundreds of concerts" he says he attended while in high school.

When he was 18, Mike took his passion for music a step further after receiving a set of drums as a present from his father. He began to pound away, eventually teaching himself how to play the instrument by banging along with his favorite songs or by watching drummers on TV. His new hobby provided another release from the stresses of baseball. "I'm an aggressive person, and I needed an outlet to vent my frustrations. You know, to hit something," Piazza said in a 1995 *Sports Illustrated for Kids* interview.

Piazza still bangs away on the drums. In fact, after becoming an established baseball star in Los Angeles in the 1990s, his celebrity status allowed him to hook up with one of his favorite bands, Anthrax, and play a song with the group on stage.

Away from the music and his schoolwork, though, making it to the major leagues was still an obsession for the metalhead jock—and his father.

HIGH SCHOOL PLAYER

In the spring of 1984, Mike tried out for the varsity team at Phoenixville High as a sophomore. Usually, a varsity team is made up of juniors and seniors. A tenth grader earning a spot is not a stretch, but it is not typical either. Varsity coach John "Doc" Kennedy, who knew Mike from Little League, asked Mike if he would consider learning to be a catcher, since the Phantoms were short on players at that position. Playing behind the plate did not interest Mike at the time. He preferred to be a first baseman, where he had been playing for years and which is a far easier position to handle. In fact, first base is the least-demanding position in baseball—it is rare for the first baseman to have to throw the ball, and he does not have to move much, either.

Mike was out of luck. Because the varsity was already stocked with juniors and seniors at first base, Coach Kennedy was left with only one choice: to cut Mike from the team and assign him to the junior varsity. Mike was not happy about the decision, but he knew that was the way competitive sports worked. Besides, he also knew he would have a better chance of being on the team next season, as an eleventh grader. Sure enough, in the spring of 1985, Mike was back at varsity tryouts. This time, first base was available for the taking, and Coach Kennedy happily assigned Mike the spot. It would prove to be an extremely wise decision.

Although Mike always believed in his abilities, he had become even more confident in his batting eye in the months leading up to his junior-year season. Certainly, hitting at home helped. One other reason may have had to do with another golden opportunity presented to him by his father in late 1984.

On a Saturday morning in the fall of that year, Mr. Piazza brought home a guest to watch Mike take his licks in the batting cage. The guest just happened to be Hall of Famer Ted Williams, the famous Boston Red Sox left fielder whose .344 lifetime batting average is seventh best in major-league history. Williams had been signing autographs at a local baseball card show, and Mr. Piazza had arranged through a mutual friend for the former slugger to stop by and offer some expert tips.

The moment was huge for Mike, as it would be for any baseball nut. "I couldn't even talk because I was so nervous," Piazza revealed to *Sports Illustrated* in July 1993. The Piazzas recorded the visit on video, and though tongue-tied, Mike was

☆ ☆ ☆ ☆ ☆ ☆
TED WILLIAMS: THE SPLENDID SPLINTER

You might get an argument if you said that Ted Williams is the greatest major-league hitter of all time. But you would certainly have enough evidence to back up your case. Williams broke into the majors in 1939 and played 19 seasons with the Boston Red Sox as a left fielder. Known as the "Splendid Splinter" because he was so skinny at first, Williams showed everyone how great he was right from the start: He batted .327 with 31 home runs and 145 RBIs as a rookie. Two years later, in 1941, he hit .406. Williams is the last big-league batter to reach the .400 mark.

Williams took a scientific approach to hitting. He used his keen eyesight, quick wrists, and patience at the plate to choose pitches he liked and knew he could hit well. He was a two-time American League Most Valuable Player (1946 and 1949). In 1942 and 1947, he won the Triple Crown of hitting by leading the league in batting average, home runs, and RBIs. Only one other player has earned the Triple Crown two times in a career: Rogers Hornsby in 1922 and 1925. Named to 17 All-Star Games, Williams led the league in batting seven times and bashed 521 career home runs despite missing nearly five full seasons while serving in the military and recovering from injuries.

Williams lacked only one major credential during his career: a World Series ring. The Red Sox earned a trip to baseball's championship just once with him in the lineup, losing to the St. Louis Cardinals in seven games in 1946. Oddly, Williams managed just 5 hits in 25 at-bats with 1 RBI in the series. The Splendid Splinter played his last game on September 28, 1960, and went out with a bang, hitting a home run in his final at-bat. He was inducted into the Hall of Fame in 1966. Four years later, he published his famous book, *The Science of Hitting*.

Boston Red Sox slugger Ted Williams crossed home plate after hitting a home run in 1960 in the final at-bat of his career. Williams watched a 16-year-old Mike Piazza hit in the Piazzas' backyard batting cage in 1984 and had encouraging words for the young player.

loose and fired up in the cage. He showed off his usual powerful stroke, driving rocket after rocket off his bat. Williams was impressed. "Mike hits it harder than I did when I was 16," Williams says on the tape. "I never saw anybody who looked better at this age."

Coming from Williams, that praise was sweeter than a goody bag from a sugar factory gift shop. Williams offered Mike advice about how to think like a hitter, including anticipating the types of pitches that might be thrown to keep him off balance, and how to work the ball and strike count. Then Williams asked if Mike had read his book, *The Science of Hitting*, a how-to manual for batters of all ages. Read it? Mike had memorized it. The excited young slugger ran upstairs and returned with his copy for Williams to sign. Inside the book, the 66-year-old Red Sox great wrote, "To Mike. Follow this book. As good as you look now, I'll be asking you for tickets [to watch you play in the majors some day]."

With Williams's sterling endorsement of his talent still in his mind, Mike lit up the varsity the following spring. He hit 12 home runs, breaking the single-season record for Phoenixville High, while batting .500 at the plate and driving in 38 runs. His terrific performance as a junior was an important milestone in his path toward trying to make it as a pro. It showed great potential for his senior season, the time in a high school player's career when major-league scouts come around to local diamonds in search of talent to draft.

Sure enough, Mike picked up the next season (1986) where he had left off. He hit 11 home runs, breaking the school's career record set by Andre Thornton, a Phoenixville High star in the 1960s, who played 14 seasons in the majors. Mike's batting average was .442, he drove in 42 runs, and he was named Most Valuable Player in his league. With those credentials, it seemed Mike was well on his way to the draft.

And yet, the scouts were not interested. Despite his big batting numbers, Mike just could not overcome the label of "slow feet/poor fielding." "One reason Mike was overlooked [was that] he only played first base and was slow," Coach Kennedy said in a 1994 *Sport* magazine article. "A lot of scouts said, 'I can find someone who can match the offensive performance with better speed.'"

Mike—and his dad—were bitterly disappointed. But they were just sidetracked in the pursuit of their dream. What they needed was another way to catch the scouts' eyes, another way into the draft. To do that, Mr. Piazza turned once again to Tommy Lasorda.

Looking to Prove Himself

Like most pro athletes today, Mike Piazza is a beefy package of thick, muscular arms, broad shoulders, and hulking torso. He is 6 feet, 3 inches tall and weighs a solid 215 pounds. That power plant of a body allows Piazza to launch baseballs over major-league fences some 400 feet (122 meters) away with apparent ease. Piazza was not always so strong. He built himself up over the early years of his major-league baseball career. When he graduated from Phoenixville High, his build was much slighter.

In 1986, with high school diploma in hand and no plans for any other career, the gawky 17-year-old was left to wonder about his baseball future. He said in a 1993 *Sports Illustrated* interview that prospects looked bleak back then. "I have talked to a lot of scouts since [high school] who said they didn't like anything about me. They said I couldn't run or hit."

Those premature scouting reports did not stop the Piazzas from leaping into action, of course. They came up with a plan to help improve Mike's prospects. Mr. Piazza figured Mike needed a chance to prove his talent playing against better competition on a bigger stage. If he could succeed, the scouts would come calling again. The bigger stage Mr. Piazza had in mind was college baseball.

Once more, Mike's father put in a call to Lasorda, who got in touch with an old friend of his, Ron Fraser, then the coach of the University of Miami (Florida) baseball team. Year after year, the Miami Hurricanes were one of the best college baseball teams in the nation. Fraser agreed to help out Lasorda and arranged for Mike to enroll in the university and join the team. At the age of 18, Mike Piazza was looking at another golden opportunity.

This time, however, the opportunity did not work out the way Piazza or his father hoped. The Hurricanes were loaded with juniors and seniors, leaving Piazza, a freshman, with little playing time. He was a backup first baseman who got up to bat just nine times and had one hit. With little chance to show his stuff, Piazza quit the team at the end of the season in 1987 and returned home, disappointed and dejected.

Piazza's baseball future looked bleak again, but his father was not ready to abandon the college plan yet. He picked up the phone and again called Lasorda. This time, the Dodgers manager dialed the number of Demie Mainieri, the coach at Miami Dade North Community College, a small, two-year Florida school known for its outstanding baseball program. Piazza transferred to Miami Dade that fall, and in the spring of 1988, stepped back onto the baseball diamond, looking to prove himself again.

This time, life on the field went better for the 19-year-old sophomore. Although an injury to his left hand cut short his season, Piazza batted a very respectable .364 and was the starting first baseman. "He showed some flashes of power," Mainieri said in the book *Mike Piazza* by Brant James. "And that was good considering our home park was 390 feet (119 meters) to the power alleys. I worked a lot with him trying to make him a very aggressive hitter, and he turned into an aggressive hitter. I think that's why he [became] so good at hitting in clutch situations."

Mainieri said in the same interview that he was also impressed with Piazza's strong throwing arm and his enthusiasm. "He was always a very positive, upbeat person. He had incredible work habits; he was always the first one out there [at practice] and the last to leave."

Despite Piazza's progress, however, the scouts did not come calling. When he returned home from school for the start of summer, he was at a crossroads in his baseball career—and his life. He could not enroll again at Miami Dade for the next season because he had used up two years of college eligibility. He had no offers to play for a larger, four-year school, like the University of Miami. He had no major-league offers. It seemed he had no baseball future at all.

Then the most golden of all golden opportunities presented itself.

HERE COME THE DODGERS

Over the years, Mr. Piazza and Tommy Lasorda had become close through their business dealings. The two men hung out together and frequently ended up talking about Mike. In a joking kind of way, they used to imagine how amazing it would be if Mike grew up to play for the Dodgers one day. Although the odds of Piazza ever playing for Los Angeles seemed paper thin by 1988, a related idea sprang to Mr. Piazza's mind: Lasorda could ask the Dodgers to select his son in the draft that June. Sure, Piazza might not be ready to play pro ball, but the attention that came with being drafted by a major-league team might make him more appealing to a four-year college in need of a power-hitting first baseman.

The Dodgers approved the plan, but team officials were not about to waste an early-round draft pick on such a raw, untested kid whom they were told to select. So they waited until the sixty-second round, after 1,389 other players had been chosen, before finally calling out the name "Michael Piazza."

Players chosen in the early rounds of the draft typically receive an immediate phone call from their new team with the news of their selection. Because Piazza was a "courtesy pick"—a late-round player chosen as a favor—the Dodgers sent him his

☆ ☆ ☆ ☆ ☆
INSIDE THE BASEBALL DRAFT

Over the last few years, the NBA and NFL drafts have become glamorous spectacles shown live on ESPN. By contrast, the major-league draft is a swift, no-nonsense affair that gets very little attention. Baseball holds its annual draft every June in a conference call with representatives from all 30 teams. They take turns making selections. The team with the lowest winning percentage from the previous season goes first, followed by the second-worst, the third-worst, and so on, and so on, until the team with the best record makes the final selection in a round. Each team has two minutes to select a player.

Back in 1988, when Mike Piazza was drafted in the sixty-second round, there was no limit on the number of rounds. Teams simply chose and chose until the players with potential were gone. Today's draft lasts 50 rounds and sometimes ends earlier. Eligible players include high school graduates who have not yet started college; players from four-year colleges who have completed their junior or senior years, or are at least 21 years old; junior college players no matter how many years of school they have completed; and anyone who is 21 or turns 21 within 45 days of the draft date.

news in a form letter that arrived the next day. They might as well have addressed the letter to "Dear 1,390." To the Dodgers, Piazza was a number, not a prospect.

Two months later, in August 1988, a Dodgers scout finally got around to contacting Piazza by phone. The call was not to negotiate a minor-league contract. It was to find out where No. 1,390 was going to college that fall so the team could follow

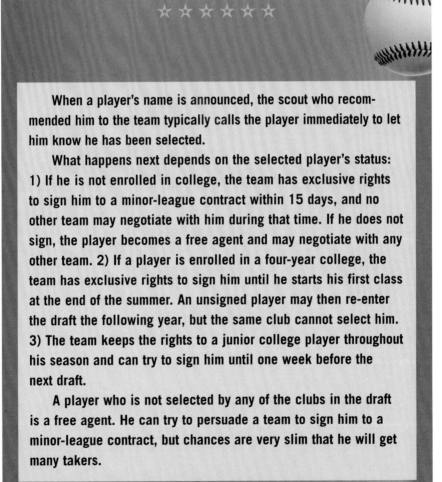

☆ ☆ ☆ ☆ ☆

When a player's name is announced, the scout who recommended him to the team typically calls the player immediately to let him know he has been selected.

What happens next depends on the selected player's status: 1) If he is not enrolled in college, the team has exclusive rights to sign him to a minor-league contract within 15 days, and no other team may negotiate with him during that time. If he does not sign, the player becomes a free agent and may negotiate with any other team. 2) If a player is enrolled in a four-year college, the team has exclusive rights to sign him until he starts his first class at the end of the summer. An unsigned player may then re-enter the draft the following year, but the same club cannot select him. 3) The team keeps the rights to a junior college player throughout his season and can try to sign him until one week before the next draft.

A player who is not selected by any of the clubs in the draft is a free agent. He can try to persuade a team to sign him to a minor-league contract, but chances are very slim that he will get many takers.

Roy Krasik, the senior director of Major League Baseball operations, monitored his computer during the amateur baseball draft on June 7, 2005. He was at the Major League Baseball offices in New York City. Unlike the glitzier drafts in pro football and basketball, which are televised, the baseball draft is a brisk affair conducted by conference call. Teams get two minutes to make a selection.

his progress. Piazza seized the moment. He requested a tryout from the team. If they could just see him hit, he figured, he would have another shot at his dream. The Dodgers agreed.

Very quickly, Piazza boarded a plane headed for the West Coast. Before he knew it, he was standing at home plate at Dodger Stadium with a bat in his hand. On the mound stood Dodgers bullpen coach Mike Cresse. Seated nearby were

Lasorda and Ben Wade, Los Angeles's scouting director. All the golden opportunities in Piazza's baseball career had come down to this one, bright, shining instant.

Boom! Boom! Boom! Just like he did when Ted Williams came to his house, Piazza lit up onstage. He crushed ball after ball deep into the outfield grass and over the fence in a fearsome display of power. "Cresse threw me good pitches," Piazza said in 1993 to *Sports Illustrated*. "I just hammered balls into the blue seats."

You can only imagine how much pride Lasorda was feeling as he watched the son of his good friend finally get to show his stuff in a major-league ballpark. Lasorda, though, also knew he had some work to do to convince Wade that the Dodgers should sign Piazza to a contract. After all, the kid could hit, that was obvious, but he still had the label of "slow runner and poor fielder" attached to his name.

Lasorda turned to Wade. "If he was a catcher who could hit balls into the seats like that, would you sign him?" asked the Dodgers manager.

"Yes," replied Wade.

"Then he's a catcher," said Lasorda.

"No he's not, he's a first baseman," Wade said stubbornly.

The scouting director did not know it, but Lasorda had had a plan for Piazza. At the end of Piazza's season with Miami Dade, Mr. Piazza and his son had discussed the possibility of Mike's learning to be a catcher. Since catchers are not expected to have quick feet and are always in demand, they figured making the switch might give Mike a better shot at the majors. In fact, Mr. Piazza and Lasorda already knew that Mike had some of the skills necessary to learn the position, thanks to a "mini-tryout" earlier in the summer arranged by Lasorda. At that tryout, Mike threw for 10 minutes with Joe Ferguson, a former catcher with the Dodgers. As stated in *Sports Illustrated* in 1993, Ferguson reported to Lasorda and Mr. Piazza afterward, "The kid's got the arm. He can be a catcher."

Lasorda talked Wade into allowing Piazza to show what he could do from behind the plate. "I threw as hard as I could," Piazza reported in the 1993 *Sports Illustrated* article. "I think my arm is still hurting from that day." Pain or no pain, Piazza's bullets to second base clinched the deal for Wade. He might have some potential. A short time later, Wade offered Piazza $15,000 to sign a minor-league contract. Piazza jumped for the pen. "I said yes before [Wade] said, 'thousand,'" Mike recalled in the *Sports Illustrated* interview. "He could have said fifteen dollars, and it wouldn't have mattered."

KINDERGARTEN FOR CATCHERS

Piazza had reached the goal he had set for himself as a boy. "I was finally a professional ballplayer," he said with pride in the 1994 *Los Angeles Times Magazine* article. Now, another huge hurdle stood before him. A catcher's job is very complex and can take years to master. Most major-league catchers start to play the position in high school, or earlier. Piazza, now 20 years old, would have to learn the ins and outs of backstopping almost from scratch. "I knew I had a tremendous amount of work to do," he said in the 1994 *Sport* magazine interview. "I knew I swung the bat well enough to get to play if I learned to catch."

Eager to start his schooling right away, Piazza took an unusual step. He volunteered to go to a training academy run by the Dodgers in the Dominican Republic, a nation located on the island of Hispaniola in the Caribbean, where Spanish is the native language. The academy was for Latin American ballplayers, but that did not matter to Piazza. "I knew I would catch every day," he said in the 1993 *Sports Illustrated* article. In late 1988, Piazza reported to Campo Las Palmas as the academy's first American-born trainee.

After growing up in the comforts of the United States, with its big houses, over-stocked supermarkets, fast food, new cars, and mega-malls, Piazza was in for a major dose of culture shock. The Dominican Republic is extremely poor, and conditions at the academy were rugged, to say the least. As stated in the Brant James book, Piazza said, "There were tarantulas," referring to the giant species of spider. "They never bit me, but you don't want to wake up with one."

For the three months Piazza was at the academy, he and his schoolmates were served the same cheap food every day: "For breakfast, two poached eggs and something I think was ham; for lunch, chicken broth and two ham sandwiches; and for dinner, beans and rice, a little bit of beef and sugarcane juice," Piazza said in the 1993 *Sports Illustrated* article. "To the Dominican kids, it was a feast."

As the only English-speaking player, Piazza felt homesick at times. The unfamiliar food often made him sick, and he wound up losing 25 pounds. In some ways, though, the experience toughened him up. The Mike Piazza who returned to Pennsylvania at Christmastime had more muscle, knew a little Spanish, and best of all, had become a better catcher.

THE MINOR LEAGUES

The next stop in Piazza's journey was the minor leagues. In June 1989, he reported to the Dodgers' Single-A Rookie team in Salem, Oregon. It was the bottom rung of the minor-league ladder. Piazza batted .268 and hit eight home runs—not remarkable but good enough to earn him a promotion the following season. Now 21 years old, he arrived in Vero Beach, Florida, in March 1990. His batting average slipped to .250, but he pounded out 20 doubles and helped the Vero Beach Dodgers win the Florida State League championship.

Although his year at Vero Beach ended on a high note, in reality, Piazza's first two seasons as a professional ballplayer showed little of the talent that was to come. Perhaps pressing to prove he belonged, he rarely relaxed enough at the plate to perform at his best. He struck out 119 times and drew just 24 walks. He also ran into some of the problems that came with being a draft pick nobody wanted who also happened to be a favorite of the big-league club's manager. Some players were resentful of his status or playing time, and mocked him. At Vero Beach, Piazza lost his starting position as catcher after three months, when he clashed with his manager, Joe Alvarez. Piazza felt that Alvarez did not respect him simply because he was a courtesy pick. "Coach didn't like my attitude," Piazza said in the *Los Angeles Times Magazine* in 1994.

Alvarez saw the situation differently. "Mike considered himself a free spirit," Alvarez said in the same article. "He had his own ideas. I had mine."

On the positive side, Piazza's catching skills were coming along. "Once I started to make some progress, I became that much more intense on trying to improve," he told *Sports Illustrated for Kids* in 1995.

Piazza began the 1991 season in Single-A ball again, this time in Bakersfield, California. It would be a turning point for him, in more ways than one. On the field, he finally unleashed the power that had been bottled up inside. He hit .277, drove in 80 runs, and smacked 29 homers, more than any other Dodger minor leaguer that year. At season's end, *Baseball America* magazine named him a Single-A all-star. He also unleashed a new attitude about the game. "I lightened up and didn't take myself so seriously," Piazza told the Web site *At the Yard* in 2004. "I stopped putting so much pressure on myself."

Suddenly, the slow-footed former first baseman known more for his relationship with Tommy Lasorda than for his talent was a genuine major-league prospect.

Eager to keep the momentum going, Piazza headed out of the country in the fall of 1991 to play for Mexicali in the Mexican Pacific League. His bat stayed red hot, and he hit .330 with 16 home runs. When he returned in 1992, the Dodgers put him on a fast track: They invited him to spring training with the big-league club in Florida. The idea was to give him a taste of the majors and get a close-up look at the kid who had lit up

Bakersfield. Then they sent the 23-year-old to the Double-A team in San Antonio, Texas. After batting .377 in his first 31 games, the Dodgers promoted Piazza to their Triple-A club in Albuquerque, New Mexico.

Piazza was just one step away from the majors. In his heart, he knew it was only a matter of time before he would be standing at home plate at Dodger Stadium again with a bat in his hands. Only this time, he would be swinging at live fastballs from a big-league pitcher with thousands of fans cheering for him. "I kind of knew in spring training when I started hitting the best of the best; that gave me a lot of confidence," he told *Stack* magazine. "When I was in [Double A], I was like, 'There is no reason why I can't be hitting big-league pitchers right now.'"

By the time the minor-league season in Albuquerque ended in late August, Piazza was king of the plate. He led the team with a .341 batting average, had blasted 16 home runs, and had hit in 25 games in a row at one point, the second-longest streak in Albuquerque history. With those numbers, it was no surprise that Piazza was voted the Dodgers' minor-league player of the year for 1992.

And it was no surprise that Piazza got the call he had hoped for since he first whacked baseballs in the basement with his dad back in Phoenixville. Late in August, the Dodgers told Piazza to catch a flight to Chicago, Illinois. They wanted him for a three-game set against the Cubs. Piazza arrived in Chicago on a standard commercial airliner, but you have to believe he could have somehow flown there under his own power. That was how excited he was.

The Rookie Arrives

Mike Piazza walked into the Dodgers' locker room at Wrigley Field in Chicago on September 1 to find a team wallowing in last place in the National League's West Division. Already out of contention for a playoff spot with a record of 54–78, Los Angeles's miserable season might have been a blessing in disguise. It meant there was less pressure for Piazza and the other September call-ups from the minors to help the team win. Instead, making it to "The Show" was about gaining experience and trying to earn a shot at winning a spot on the roster the following spring training.

Generally speaking, one game does not make or break a player's career. One game, however, can make a big statement, and that is exactly what Piazza did in his first appearance in a big-league game. With his dad watching proudly from the

stands, Piazza stroked a fourth-inning double in his first official turn at bat. After singling in the sixth inning, and adding
another single in the eighth, Piazza finished the day a perfect
three for three. To top it off, he threw out Chicago's Dwight
Smith on an attempted steal of second in the fifth inning. The
Dodgers won the game, 5-4, in 13 innings.

You could hardly have scripted a better beginning. "A
couple of times I looked around and said, 'I can't believe this
is happening,'" Piazza said afterward to a *Los Angeles Times*
reporter. Meanwhile, Manager Tommy Lasorda gushed to the
San Francisco Chronicle on September 2: "To see him hitting
all those thousands of balls at an early age, to see him pay the
price, to see his dream finally come true . . . it was a great day."

Eleven days later, on September 12, Piazza launched his first
major-league home run, a fifth-inning, three-run blast off of
San Francisco Giants pitcher Steve Reed in a 7-0 Dodgers win.
All told, Piazza appeared in 21 games for Los Angeles in 1992,
with 69 at-bats. Although he finished with just one homer and
an unexceptional batting average of .232, his presence behind
the plate and his potential for power had the Dodgers coaches
talking. When the season ended, Piazza could not wait to put
on a baseball uniform again. In October, he packed up his gear
and reported to the Arizona Fall League, a showcase for top
rookies and minor leaguers who want to polish, and showcase,
their skills. And showcase he did: Piazza batted .291, with three
home runs and 23 runs batted in for the Sun Cities Solar Sox.

It had been a spectacular year: From Double A to Triple A
to the majors in one season. Few players travel so quickly up
the baseball ladder.

FIRST FULL SEASON

There was good news waiting for Piazza at Dodgertown, Los
Angeles's spring-training complex in Vero Beach, Florida, in
February 1993: The starting catcher's job was up for grabs.

Mike Piazza is pictured here at bat on September 13, 1992, during a game against the San Francisco Giants. Piazza started the season playing Double-A ball for the Dodgers' minor-league team in San Antonio, Texas. He was promoted to the Triple-A team and then was called up to the majors in September.

Over the winter, the Dodgers had released Mike Scioscia, their first-stringer of the previous 13 seasons. Piazza would be competing with Carlos Hernandez, a backup catcher for the past three seasons who had played in only 94 games, and Lance Parrish, a 16-year veteran nearing the end of his career.

It turned out to be a one-man race. The Dodgers finished the 1992 season with the fewest home runs (72) in the National League, and they were looking to upgrade their offense. Hernandez and Parrish were known more for their defense. Piazza's big bat delivered the goods during the spring exhibition season. He hit .478 with 4 home runs, 1 triple, 4 doubles, and 11 RBIs. His eye-popping power wowed his teammates, who frequently dropped their gloves to gather around the batting cage and watch him crush baseballs high into the Florida air.

Piazza's awesome spring stats made Lasorda's decision to name his starting catcher for 1993 a no-brainer. "I don't want to brag about [Mike], but he really was a shining star in camp," Lasorda told the *Los Angeles Times* in 1993. "He has worked hard." Piazza's performance also helped keep the doubters off both their backs. No one could accuse Lasorda of giving his 24-year-old rookie the starter's job just because he was a family friend.

Piazza also delivered the goods on defense. His footwork and his throwing accuracy greatly improved. The rookie's development behind the plate was due in large part to his perseverance but also to his willingness to listen to the advice he received from his coaches, including Roy Campanella, one of the best all-around catchers of all time. Campanella had been a star of the great Brooklyn Dodgers teams of the late 1940s and early '50s. (The Dodgers moved to Los Angeles in 1958.) He was the real deal: a three-time Most Valuable Player blessed with cat-quick reflexes and a rifle arm (not to mention a booming bat) who played in five World Series. In 1955, he helped Brooklyn win its only championship.

Tragically, Campanella's career was cut short when he was paralyzed in a car wreck in 1958. Though confined to a wheelchair for the rest of his life, each spring he tutored the young Dodger catchers in the fundamentals of the position. Piazza soaked up his wisdom, including the need to practice the same moves over and over, no matter how boring. "[Campanella] told me, 'You don't want to get into a situation where you ask, What do I have to do?' " Piazza told *USA Today* in 1993. "You just want to do it."

When the regular season began on April 6, Piazza was still blazing hot. He threw out 11 of 15 runners trying to steal. At the plate, he won the National League Player of the Week honor in late April, collecting 10 hits in 23 trips to the plate, with four home runs and eight runs batted in. He would win the award two more times, once in June and again in September.

With all cylinders on the Piazza machine primed to run smoothly in 1993, baseball life seemed pretty sweet. Unlike his days back in Single A, though, Piazza found it difficult to relax and enjoy his success. He drove himself hard, almost as if he were scared to fail. His teammates began to call him "snapper" because of his intensity and the way he would suddenly snap at times and become upset with his play on the field. In a May 31 game against the St. Louis Cardinals, for example, Piazza made a funny mistake, but to him it was no laughing matter. With pitcher Tom Candiotti on the mound for the Dodgers, Piazza lunged for a pitch out of the strike zone, snared it, and then threw off balance toward second, hoping to snag a runner trying to steal. The throw hit Candiotti instead—on the rear end. The Los Angeles infielders and outfielders cracked up. Piazza, though, started to curse. He was angry at himself and embarrassed. "He takes everything so seriously," teammate Eric Karros told *Sports Illustrated* in 1993. "We were winning 5-0, so who cares? . . . It was funny."

The next day the Dodger pitchers appeared at the ballpark wearing targets on the seats of their pants. It was a classic comedy

Despite being paralyzed in a 1958 car accident, Dodgers great Roy Campanella turned out for spring training each year to guide the team's young catchers. Here, he offered some pointers at Dodgertown in Vero Beach, Florida, in March 1980. Campanella taught Mike Piazza the value of repetition in training.

moment in baseball, a sport with a long tradition of outrageous pranks and teasing, but Piazza was not amused. "He still felt pretty bad about it," Candiotti said. "He said to me, 'What if I had hit you in the arm?' Catching is not a casual thing for him. If I lose a game, he feels like he let me down." It would take a few years for Piazza to learn to control his temper on the field and not take things so personally.

Besides the pressure that Piazza put on himself to be perfect, another issue was keeping him from basking in his success. In the previous year, Piazza's father had put together a plan with a group of investors to try to buy the San Francisco Giants. They hoped to move the Giants to St. Petersburg, Florida. It was an important sports story, and in some ways it overshadowed Piazza's own dramatic story. Even after his marvelous three-for-three debut game, some reporters had asked Piazza about his father's plan. They wanted to know if Mr. Piazza was going to name Lasorda as manager of the St. Petersburg club.

Nine days after Piazza's debut, the Major League Baseball team owners turned down Mr. Piazza's offer. One reported reason was that two members of the investors' group had failed background security checks. The rejection angered Mr. Piazza, and he filed a lawsuit against Major League Baseball the following December, claiming that the owners had discriminated against him. The suit was still being reviewed in 1993 even as Piazza was bashing fastballs over the fences at Dodger Stadium. (Major League Baseball eventually paid Mr. Piazza's group $6 million to settle the suit and sent a letter of apology.) Seeing his father's name in the newspapers and being questioned about the lawsuit were distracting and irritating to Piazza.

Another issue also caused the rookie some trouble. A rumor had begun during spring training that Piazza was the godson of the Dodgers manager. In truth, that honor went to Piazza's youngest brother, Tommy. For some reason, though, Piazza and Lasorda did not bother to set the record straight for a number of months. That kept the issue of Piazza's qualifications for his job an open subject, and a few reporters would not let it go. "Like I don't deserve to be here?" Piazza said to a *Sports Illustrated* reporter in 1993. "Like [Lasorda's] doing me a favor by letting me on the team? Like all of this [success] was done with mirrors?" Despite all the nonsense, Piazza managed to keep his concentration where it mattered most: on the field.

FIRST-TIME ALL-STAR

As the halfway point of the 1993 season neared, it was obvious that the Dodgers had a genuine rookie phenom on their roster.

In late June, Piazza was ranked among the top 10 in the National League in five offensive categories, including: batting average (.331), home runs (15), and runs batted in (52). He also had 11 game-winning RBIs. His incredible stats helped catapult the Dodgers into third place in the National League's West Division.

Piazza's enormous talent was obvious to baseball fans, too, who cast their votes for the newcomer to join the National League team at the All-Star Game. Piazza led the Dodgers in home runs (18) by the time the sixty-fourth midseason classic rolled around on July 13, and he had thrown out 38 of 98 runners trying to steal. The All-Star selection was a huge honor. "I'm glad the people more or less see that I belong here because I've worked at it and I've done the job," he told the *New York Times* that year.

The 1993 All-Star Game took place at Camden Yards in Baltimore, Maryland, home of the Orioles. Piazza was invited to participate in the traditional home-run derby held the day before the big game. Unfortunately, he did not perform up to his high standards. Competing against superstars like Barry Bonds and Ken Griffey, Jr., Piazza failed to jack a single homer out of the park. Juan González of the Texas Rangers won the event with seven homers. Perhaps Piazza felt tense or intimidated on such a grand stage so early in his career. If so, the discomfort carried over into the All-Star Game the next night, when he struck out in his only turn at bat.

Whatever embarrassment Piazza might have felt about his All-Star experience, however, did not affect him in the second half of the season. He continued on his torrid pace, hitting .320 the rest of the way, while adding another 17 home runs. At season's end, his final stats blew everyone away, and he was chosen National League Rookie of the Year in a unanimous vote by the Baseball Writers' Association of America. Again, it was a one-man race: His .318 batting average was the highest of any National League Rookie of the Year since the award began in 1947. His 112 RBIs made him the first award winner to drive

Mike Piazza waited to catch a pop-up during a game on July 25, 1993, against the New York Mets at Dodger Stadium. Piazza finished his first full season with a .318 batting average and 35 home runs. He was named the National League Rookie of the Year.

in 100 runs or more. His home run total (35) set a record for first-year catchers and was the third-highest all-time total for any National League rookie. Piazza also threw out 58 runners, the most in the majors that year.

On the evening of the awards ceremony, Piazza went on a thanking spree. Everyone made the list: his parents, the fans, Tommy Lasorda, his teammates, and Roy Campanella, who had passed away on June 26 at the age of 71. Afterward, Piazza told a reporter from the *Los Angeles Times*, "This is definitely at the top to win this award. I look at the tremendous players who have won this award, and, well, it's just now starting to sink in."

Though the star performer did not get to take a bow for winning the trophy, he did have a chance to bask in the glow of the fans' admiration at Dodger Stadium on the last day of the season. After pounding out two home runs and knocking in four runs in a 12-1 victory against the San Francisco Giants, the home crowd gave Piazza three standing ovations. He popped back out of the dugout to tip his cap. The victory over the Dodgers' archrival was doubly special: It gave Los Angeles a final record of 81–81, an improvement of 18 wins over 1992, and it knocked San Francisco out of the playoffs.

Piazza capped off the season by traveling to Asia with the Dodgers to play a series of exhibition games against pro teams in Taiwan and Japan. The new superstar showed some American muscle in the first game when he bashed a home run against Taiwan in a 4-2 Dodgers win.

For Piazza, 1993 had been a storybook season. Besides being named top rookie, he won the Silver Slugger award, given to the best hitting player at each position. His peers also started to notice his extraordinary power. One blast stood out: a line-drive rocket over the center-field wall at Riverfront Stadium in Cincinnati, Ohio, home of the Reds. The homer on June 20 was measured at 436 feet (133 meters), but the players and writers who saw it that day said the ball traveled at least 500 feet (152 meters), maybe even 550 feet (168 meters).

"I've seen fly balls get to that part of the park, but not line drives," said his teammate Eric Davis, a former center fielder for the Reds. "That guy is from another planet."

☆ ☆ ☆ ☆ ☆ ☆

ROOKIES OF THE YEAR

The first Rookie of the Year award was handed out in 1947. It went to Jackie Robinson, the great Brooklyn Dodgers infielder who broke baseball's color barrier that year. (The trophy was officially renamed the Jackie Robinson Award in 1987.) Only one player from the majors was named top newcomer in the first two years of the award. Starting in 1949, two players won the trophy—one from the National League and one from the American League.

Winning the Rookie of the Year award is a huge honor, but it does not guarantee a successful career. Does anyone remember Bob Hamelin? The shortstop for the 1994 Kansas City Royals was named the top rookie in the American League that season. He hit 24 home runs and batted .282. By 1998, he was stumbling through his final season in the big leagues, done in by injuries and fading talent. His lifetime batting average: .246. On the other side of the coin, some rookies have soared after winning the award. Derek Jeter of the New York Yankees won the 1996 trophy in the American League. He has a lifetime batting average of .317 after 12 major-league seasons—and four World Series championships.

Only two Rookies of the Year have been named Most Valuable Player in the same year: Fred Lynn of the Boston Red Sox in 1975 and Ichiro Suzuki of the Seattle Mariners in 2001. In 1981, Rookie of the Year winner Fernando Valenzuela, a pitcher with the Los Angeles Dodgers, also earned the Cy Young Award.

Here's a look at some amazing Rookie of the Year winners, the season they won, and some of their notable career achievements.

"[He] hits balls as hard as anyone I've ever seen," Dodger batting coach Reggie Smith told *USA Today* in 1994. "That includes [Hall of Fame superstars Hank] Aaron, [Willie] Mays,

☆ ☆ ☆ ☆ ☆

Player	Rookie Season	Achievements
Willie Mays New York Giants	1951	National League MVP in 1954 and 1965; slugged 660 home runs, fourth-most all time.
Johnny Bench Cincinnati Reds	1968	One of the game's best all-around catchers; National League MVP in 1970 and 1972.
Mark McGwire Oakland A's	1987	Only Rookie of the Year to also lead the league in home runs (49) in the same season.
Ichiro Suzuki Seattle Mariners	2001	His .350 batting average led the league in his Rookie of the Year season.
Albert Pujols St. Louis Cardinals	2001	First major leaguer to hit 30 or more home runs in each of his first six seasons.

[Willie] McCovey, [Willie] Stargell. He even makes his own holes on ground balls."

"In my 13 years I haven't seen anybody hit the ball as hard and as far consistently," teammate Brett Butler told the *San Francisco Chronicle* in 1993.

Piazza was flattered by the compliments. He also knew, though, that it was important to keep the success from going to his head. He was aware that many rookies had seen their careers crash and burn after just one season in the bigs. Call it the sophomore jinx. Piazza was determined to match his high standards in 1994. He told the *Los Angeles Times* in 1993:

> I am proud that no matter what I have done, I have strived to improve. No matter what happens in the future for me, I have to keep the same attitude. I can't just sit back on my laurels and say that I've arrived and don't have to work anymore. Now that I've established myself as a pretty good hitter, [teams] will be gunning for me that much more.

Hall of Fame catcher Yogi Berra, a three-time MVP with the New York Yankees, was as superstitious as anyone in baseball about the sophomore jinx. When asked by the *Los Angeles Times Magazine* in 1994 about Piazza's prospects for the upcoming season, Berra said, "Now we'll see what this Piazza kid's made of."

True Stardom

Although Mike Piazza had only one full season of major-league play under his belt, his life changed dramatically after winning the Rookie of the Year award in 1993. Suddenly, he was a star, with all the demands that came with fame. Fans who wanted autographs were drawn to him when he went out in public, including one kid who followed him through Los Angeles International Airport calling out his name repeatedly. "Stardom is a strange thing," Piazza told *Sport* magazine in May 1994. "Being recognized is something I've never had to deal with before." Sportswriters and TV reporters wanted his opinions, and charities asked for his time to help promote their causes. Piazza tried to oblige. He gladly signed his name when he could, answered questions patiently, and visited hospitals to cheer up sick children.

Piazza's fame, though, went beyond baseball, for he was a star in the land of stars: Los Angeles, California. In the off-season, the 25-year-old bachelor, living in a town house in the Los Angeles suburb of Manhattan Beach, took in all that the glamorous city had to offer. He sat courtside at Los Angeles Lakers games and rinkside to watch the NHL's Los Angeles Kings. He shot a TV commercial for a baseball card company and swung for the fences in the third annual MTV Rock n' Jock celebrity softball game. He also took to the road, traveling to Las Vegas, Nevada, to watch high-profile boxing matches.

The dramatic changes in his life carried over into spring training as well. When Piazza pulled into Vero Beach in February 1994, it was the first time in his professional baseball career that he would not have to prove his talent to keep his place on a team. The starting catcher's job was his. He was also the proud owner of a new three-year contract from the Dodgers worth $4.2 million, a record amount awarded to a player entering his second season in the big leagues.

THE BASEBALL STRIKE OF 1994

The Dodgers were an upbeat bunch in early 1994. They returned their superb starting pitching staff from the year before, a collection of right-handers who had finished with the third-lowest earned-run average (3.50) in the majors (thanks in part to Piazza's excellent pitch-calling from behind the plate). A 20-year-old rookie hurler with nasty stuff named Chan Ho Park was in camp, trying to become the first pitcher from South Korea to make it to the majors. The Dodgers' hitting looked to be even better with promising new slugger Raul Mondesi joining Piazza and Eric Karros, the 1992 Rookie of the Year.

The regular season, though, began slowly for the Dodgers. At the end of April, the team had a so-so record of 11–12. Luckily, the other three teams in the National League West—the Giants, the Colorado Rockies, and the San Diego Padres—were not exactly burning it up either, and Los Angeles found itself in second place, just one game behind San Francisco. By mid-May, however, all the parts began to mesh. After winning 9 of 10 games, Los Angeles took over first place on May 20, and the team's .286 batting average was third best in the National League.

If there was such a thing as a sophomore jinx, it did not exist in Piazza's world. He batted .386 in May, to go along with six homers and 24 RBIs, and he was co-winner of the National League's Player of the Month award with Philadelphia's Lenny Dykstra. He hit his first career grand slam on June 6 off of Florida Marlins pitcher Mark Gardner, and he belted homers in four straight games, from June 25 to 28. Once again, the fans rewarded him with a trip to the All-Star Game on July 12. This time, he was the National League's starter behind the plate, and his performance improved. He had a single in four trips to the plate and drove in a run, helping the National League to an 8-7 win. Twelve days later, his batting average stood at a robust .328.

And then it all came to a sudden, awful stop.

On August 12, acting baseball commissioner Bud Selig broke the news that fans had feared all season: The players were going on strike. Unhappy with the proposed terms of a new labor agreement presented by the team owners over the past six months, the players hung up their uniforms and walked out to express their discontent. Day after day, games were canceled even as the two sides continued to try to work out their differences. Finally, on September 14, Selig decided to cancel the rest of the regular season, plus the playoffs and the World Series. No major-league champion would be crowned for the first time in 90 years.

It was a disaster. There had been seven work stoppages by players or owners in the past, but nothing like this. Players' stats were frozen in time, owners lost money without ticket sales, and worst of all, fans were angry and confused. They wondered

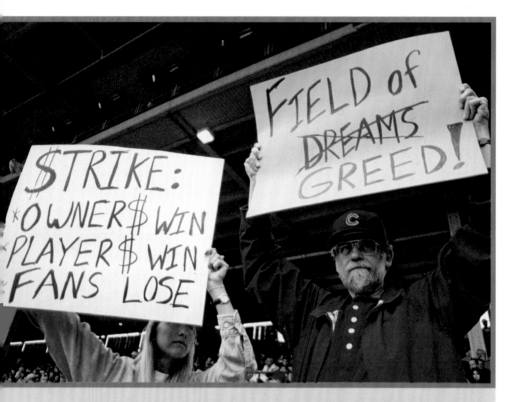

Fans at Wrigley Field in Chicago held up signs on August 10, 1994, to protest a possible baseball strike. Two days later, the players went on strike. The walkout led to the cancellation of the World Series that year and did not end until the following season.

how millionaire owners and players could act so greedily and ruin the grand tradition of a professional sport dating back more than 100 years.

Like everyone, Piazza felt the frustration and disappointment of a season cut short. He finished 1994 as the team leader in batting average (.319), home runs (24), and RBIs (92), and won his second straight National League Silver Slugger award. It was small consolation, though. He ached to be on the diamond.

To burn off some steam, he spent hours working out in the gym. He had begun to lift weights seriously in 1991 as a minor leaguer, to build up his strength at the plate and to improve his endurance behind it. "[Lifting] makes me feel strong, powerful . . . tough," he told the *Los Angeles Times Magazine* in 1994. Piazza packed muscle onto muscle over those three years, until his playing weight in 1994 reached 215 pounds (97.5 kilograms). His chiseled shoulders, arms, and chest made him look like an indestructible robo-catcher. Piazza also used the downtime from the strike to try out his acting skills in Hollywood. He appeared in a soap opera and on two popular nighttime shows: the sitcom *Married With Children,* and the beach drama *Baywatch.* Back at his home in Manhattan Beach, he tried to work out his anger over the lost season by thrashing away on his drums.

BRING BACK THE FANS!

The strike dragged on into 1995. By February, the joy normally found around the opening of spring training was missing. Dodgertown was as quiet as a library. Or worse, a morgue. The team owners, wanting to make money and trying to please fans, invited minor leaguers to come to camp and play in exhibition games. The fans were not fooled. They saw through the scheme and barely turned out. They wanted the real deal: major-league stars.

Meanwhile, the big leaguers tried to stay sharp in preparation for the day the strike would end. Piazza worked out with buddies from the Montreal Expos and the Boston Red Sox at a training complex in Delray Beach, Florida. They took batting practice and worked on their fielding and throwing. But it just was not the same. "I miss spring training and all the fans that stop you on your way to the games. I miss the locker room jokes on the rookies . . . and Tommy [Lasorda], the ringmaster in his golf cart," Piazza told *Sports Illustrated* in March 1995.

As February rolled into March, it became clear that the owners and players would not be able to settle their dispute on their own. When the owners voted to begin the regular season using replacement players, a federal judge stepped in. She issued an order forcing the owners to continue the work rules of the expired labor agreement. After the judge's order, the players' union offered on April 2 to play without a new agreement, ending the strike. The walkout had lasted 232 days and resulted in the cancellation of 938 games.

The 1995 season was cut back from its normal 162 games to 144, and Opening Day was set for April 25. The fans, though, were still fuming. On the first day of the season, three men wearing T-shirts with the word *Greed* written across the front

☆ ☆ ☆ ☆ ☆
GREAT BASEBALL MOVIES

Major League Baseball and the movies grew up around the same time—in the early twentieth century. So it was only natural for the two forms of popular entertainment to come together at some point. The earliest baseball movies were short films with little or no story. They were shot during the silent era before movies had sound, and they mostly featured the stars of the game demonstrating their talents. In time, the films began to include drama, tension, and excitement—the very qualities of a baseball game. One example is *Heading Home*, a comedy/drama made in 1920. It starred Babe Ruth playing himself in the story of his rise from rags to riches.

Mike Piazza has mostly acted in TV shows. In 2002, he made his big-screen debut in the comedy *Two Weeks Notice* starring Sandra Bullock and Hugh Grant. Like Ruth, Piazza played himself. *Two Weeks Notice* is not a baseball movie, but you can catch Piazza in a scene with the two stars at Shea Stadium.

These five baseball films are among the best ever made and are worth checking out:

jumped out of the stands at Shea Stadium in New York and threw dollar bills at the players. In Pittsburgh, fans tossed sticks onto the field. The players felt the sting of the fans' rage, knowing full well they had damaged the ancient trust that existed between themselves and their customers.

For Piazza and the Dodgers, the strike was just the beginning of a most unusual season. Piazza exploded out of the gate, batting .537 with four home runs in the first three weeks of the season. But he tore ligaments in his left thumb in a game against the Padres and was placed on the disabled list from May 11 to

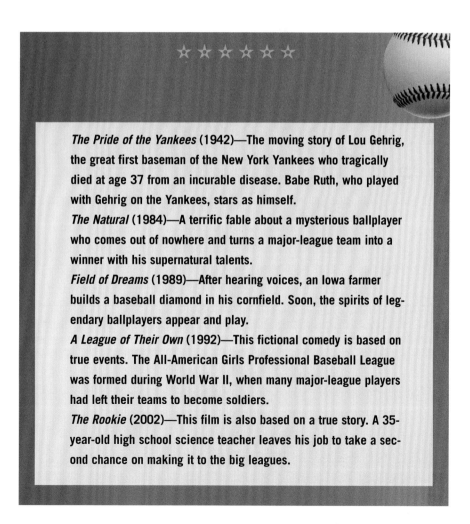

☆ ☆ ☆ ☆ ☆

The Pride of the Yankees (1942)—The moving story of Lou Gehrig, the great first baseman of the New York Yankees who tragically died at age 37 from an incurable disease. Babe Ruth, who played with Gehrig on the Yankees, stars as himself.

The Natural (1984)—A terrific fable about a mysterious ballplayer who comes out of nowhere and turns a major-league team into a winner with his supernatural talents.

Field of Dreams (1989)—After hearing voices, an Iowa farmer builds a baseball diamond in his cornfield. Soon, the spirits of legendary ballplayers appear and play.

A League of Their Own (1992)—This fictional comedy is based on true events. The All-American Girls Professional Baseball League was formed during World War II, when many major-league players had left their teams to become soldiers.

The Rookie (2002)—This film is also based on a true story. A 35-year-old high school science teacher leaves his job to take a second chance on making it to the big leagues.

June 4. He returned for a home game against the Mets and did what he does best: He homered to help the Dodgers win, 5-3. His torrid hitting continued, and by mid-June, his batting average was an astronomical .402. Soon, fans were buzzing about the possibility of Piazza's becoming the first catcher to win the league batting title since 1942.

At the same time, another Dodger was creating a sensation on the mound. Hideo Nomo, a 26-year-old rookie from Japan's professional league, was mowing down batters as if they were Little Leaguers. He was a treat to watch, with his dazzling fastball and a twisting, dizzying windup that made him look like a tornado spinning toward home plate. "Nomomania" gripped Los Angeles and Japan. By the end of June, "The Tornado" had a record of 6–1 and led the league in strikeouts (109), earning him a spot in that season's All-Star Game. Piazza joined him for his third trip to the Midsummer Classic. Named as starters, Nomo threw two innings to his Dodger battery mate, giving up only one hit while striking out three. Piazza did what he could for the overmatched National League: He threw out a runner trying to steal second, and he belted a seventh-inning, game-tying home run, one of only three hits his side managed in a losing effort.

Piazza continued to scorch opposing pitchers in the second half of the season. He had a 16-game hitting streak from July 29 to August 16, and he was named the National League's Player of the Week for August 21 to 27. It was his second Player of the Week award that season (the first was in May) and the sixth of his career.

Yet not everyone in the Los Angeles clubhouse was happy with the catcher's work. The grumbling started in late August, when the Dodgers' pitching staff was shelled for 33 runs while losing three in a row to the Phillies. Piazza committed an error in all three games. With Los Angeles clinging to first place in the National League West by just a half game, the idea of moving the slugger to another position with less responsibility became the topic of discussion among reporters covering the team.

Mike Piazza and Los Angeles Dodgers pitcher Hideo Nomo shook hands after Nomo's performance in an August 1995 game against the San Francisco Giants. Nicknamed "The Tornado" because of his windup, Nomo enthralled fans in Los Angeles during his rookie season.

It was completely ridiculous to blame Piazza for the team's woes. But the questions about his ability to call for the right kind of pitch and handle the chores of a catcher were tough to shake for someone still learning the position. The whispers about his defensive liabilities would dog him throughout his career. "I know there are times when I'm not great behind the plate," he told the *Los Angeles Times* in August 1995 after the losing streak. "It's fatiguing being behind the plate every game, but because of my bat, they can't afford to take me out of the lineup too often. . . . You keep hearing that they want to move me to a different position one day, and that would be fine. It just depends on what the Dodgers have in mind for my future."

The next day he got the critics off his back with a classic Piazza performance: He had four hits in four trips to the plate against the Phillies, with two doubles and two home runs, one a grand slam. The Dodgers won, 9-1.

On September 30, Los Angeles clinched the National League West title with a 7-2 win over the Padres in San Diego. Piazza leaped into the arms of relief pitcher Todd Worrell after the last out and began to celebrate the team's first postseason appearance since 1988. Unfortunately, the joy did not last long. The Cincinnati Reds swept the Dodgers in three games in the National League Division Series.

At baseball's annual postseason awards ceremony, Piazza once again picked up the Silver Slugger award, the third of his career. He had batted .346 for the season, second best in the National League. His average tied him with Tommy Davis for the highest single-season mark in Los Angeles Dodgers history. He swatted 32 home runs and added 93 RBIs.

It had been a roller-coaster season for Piazza and the Dodgers. At times they played brilliantly. At others, they stunk up the field. Nomo won the Rookie of the Year award, giving the Dodgers their fourth such award winner in a row. With the strike issues settled and the superb pitching staff set to return, the Dodgers looked forward to more stability and consistency in 1996—and to going deeper into the playoffs.

Top Dodger

Four weeks into spring training in 1996, Mike Piazza was hard at work on the field as usual. He was also doing his best to please his fans, spending about an hour outside the Dodgers' clubhouse one day autographing everything in sight. Piazza had become like a folk hero to many people for making it big despite the odds stacked against him. Like many major leaguers after the strike, he also saw the personal contact between players and the fans as an opportunity to help rebuild baseball's tarnished image. Still, attention did not always make him comfortable. He told the *Los Angeles Times* in March 1994: "I enjoy the people, but sometimes there are just a few bad eggs that ruin it for everybody. They don't understand I have to get my work done first. That's what brought me to this position."

When the season opened, the Dodgers found themselves back on board the roller coaster. Piazza fell into a brief power slump in the first 2½ weeks, appearing 55 times at the plate without a home run or any other extra-base hit. On May 7, the team's scrappy spark plug, center fielder Brett Butler, revealed that he had throat cancer and was leaving baseball for good to receive treatment. Then, on May 28, Piazza tore cartilage in his right knee sliding into second against the Phillies and was forced to miss a number of games. The timing could not have been worse: He was the top hitter in the National League at the time with a .373 batting average, and he was leading the Dodgers in homers (13) and RBIs (39).

Perhaps worse, as Piazza said, the tired talk began again about moving him to another position to spare him from the physical abuses a catcher's body goes through almost every game—the foul balls that ricochet off the fingers, the wild pitches that send him scrambling after the ball, the horrific home-plate collisions that leave him feeling as if a herd of dinosaurs had run him over. By playing somewhere else on the field, the logic went, Piazza could avoid wearing down his body so quickly and possibly extend his career. "Everybody brings that up," Piazza told the *Los Angeles Times* that month. "If my career is cut short because of being a catcher, so be it. If it's 10 years. So be it."

Piazza put the chatter behind him when he returned to the lineup and got busy. He hit three home runs and knocked in six runs in just five at-bats on June 29 against the Rockies. There was his marvelous performance at the All-Star Game in Philadelphia when he drove in two runs and hit a second-inning homer en route to winning the game's MVP award. All that good stuff, though, would take a backseat to the big news out of the Dodgers organization on July 29: Tommy Lasorda was stepping down as manager after 21 seasons.

Lasorda had missed a month of games after suffering a mild heart attack in late June. Concerned for his health, the

Tommy Lasorda *(right)* shook hands with Tommy Piazza, the youngest brother of Mike Piazza *(left)*, following a news conference in July 1996 at which Lasorda announced his retirement as manager of the Los Angeles Dodgers. With them was Dodgers player Eric Karros. Lasorda stepped down after more than two decades as manager. "I'm kind of stunned right now," Mike Piazza told reporters during the news conference.

68-year-old dugout leader felt it was best to give up the high-stress job of managing. "For me to get into a uniform again—as excitable as I am—I could not [manage] without being the way I am," he told the *New York Times* in July. The change was huge. Los Angeles was one of baseball's most storied and popular franchises, and Lasorda represented a link to the past when the Dodgers played in Brooklyn. Known for "bleeding Dodger blue," the loyal Norristown native had taken over the manager's position in September 1976, succeeding Walter Alston, who had held the job for the previous 23 seasons dating all the way back to 1954. Having just two managers in 43-plus seasons was a remarkable feat and spoke volumes about how the team owners, the O'Malleys, felt about the Dodgers and their players. They were like a family.

Piazza sobbed several times during Lasorda's press conference announcing the change. "I'm kind of stunned right now," he told the *New York Times*. Everyone knew what Lasorda meant to him and his success, and he preferred to let his emotions and past comments speak for themselves.

Under new manager Bill Russell, the rest of Los Angeles's season went just as it had in the earlier months: up and down. Piazza had a 19-game hitting streak from August 22 to September 12, batting .418 with three homers. On September 6, Brett Butler surprised everyone by returning to the team from throat surgery. His courage gave the team a boost in spirit, especially when he scored the winning run in his first game back. Regrettably, his season ended on September 10, when a pitch broke his hand as he was trying to bunt. Seven days later, pitcher Hideo Nomo threw a no-hitter against the Rockies in Colorado with Piazza behind the plate. Nomo was full of praise for his catcher afterward: "[Mike] called a great game," Nomo told the *Los Angeles Times* on September 19. "He gave me the right signs. He makes me feel very comfortable, very confident when I pitch."

The Dodgers lost their last three games of the season at home against the Padres and wound up in second place in the National League West, with a record of 90 wins and 72 losses. It was still good enough to earn them a trip to the playoffs as the National League's wild-card entry. But the Atlanta Braves and their dominant pitching staff held Los Angeles to a puny .147 team batting average and swept the Dodgers out of the postseason in three straight games. It was a disappointing finish, but considering the emotional upheavals the team had gone through, there was reason for pride.

As for Piazza personally, the usual hardware awaited him at season's end. He won his fourth Silver Slugger trophy as the best offensive player at his position. His .336 batting average was second best in the National League. He hit 36 homers and drove in 105 runs. He also finished second in the voting for league MVP behind San Diego's Ken Caminiti. Those impressive accomplishments, when added to his earlier ones, had been important keys to the Dodgers' success, of course, and they also put Piazza in a powerful position. The three-year contract he signed after his first season had expired, making him a free agent, and he knew the Dodgers would have to offer him a new contract with a big raise—if they wanted to keep him from possibly jumping to another team. Piazza's bargaining chips were piled high: The 28-year-old slugger had the best career batting average (.326) in Dodger history, and his 128 homers and 409 RBIs were the most of any catcher in his first four seasons in the majors. He had also helped guide Los Angeles's 1996 pitching staff to the lowest ERA (3.48) in the major leagues.

Before contract talks could start, though, there was more baseball to be played. In November, Piazza and a team of elite major leaguers, including Barry Bonds, Alex Rodriguez, and Hideo Nomo, traveled to Japan to take on a group of stars from Japan's pro league in an eight-game series. With Nomomania still raging in the pitcher's home country, he was the star attraction. Piazza also drew huge ovations for being Nomo's catcher and teammate.

Back home after the series, the negotiations for a new contract between Piazza's agent and the O'Malleys dragged into the following January. Piazza felt disappointed and frustrated at times. More and more, the O'Malleys seemed reluctant to offer big bucks to top free agents, a crucial piece of any team's plan for success. Piazza said he felt almost as if he were snubbed by his "family," as he called the Dodgers organization. That family feel was due to change soon, however: On January 6, the O'Malleys announced that they were putting the team up for sale. For now, though, Piazza was eager to get the deal done in time for spring training so he could focus on his job.

The two sides finally reached an agreement on January 21, and it was a blockbuster: two years at $15 million, making Piazza the highest-paid catcher in the business. Piazza learned of the deal while working out in the gym and immediately called his parents back in Pennsylvania. At the news conference to announce the signing, he hugged Lasorda, who was now working for the Dodgers as a vice president. "I've come a long way," Piazza told the *Los Angeles Times* on January 22. "This is still hard for me to believe. It's like a dream." With a new contract in his pocket, and Los Angeles's two straight years of

☆ ☆ ☆ ☆ ☆
WHAT IS THE "MODERN ERA" OF BASEBALL?

The roots of today's major leagues date back to 1876, when the National League (NL) was formed. Eight teams joined the league that season, including the Cincinnati Reds, the only remaining original team that has kept its name to this day. For the next 25 years, the NL was the only major league in the country. All other teams were in the minors.

In 1901, a group of minor-league owners launched the American League (AL) and began to compete with the National League for the best players in the country. At a time when the top salary for an NL player was $2,400 a year, AL owners offered as much as $6,000 per year and lured away stars like pitcher Cy Young (who would become the majors' all-time leader in victories playoff experience in the bank, Piazza and the Dodgers could now set their sights on winning a World Series.

RELUCTANT TEAMMATES

The 1997 major-league season is best remembered for three events. Interleague games were played for the first time and proved to be a fan favorite. The crowds loved the novelty of the instant rivalries created when American League and National League teams—sometimes from the same state or even city—faced each other. The second big event occurred in the postseason when the surprising Florida Marlins won the World Series only five years after their creation. The expansion team made history by winning a championship in the shortest amount of time.

Perhaps the most significant happening that year was baseball's celebration of the fiftieth anniversary of Jackie Robinson's

★ ☆ ★ ☆ ★ ☆

with 511), second baseman Napoleon Lajoie, and slugging left fielder Ed Delahanty.

The rival leagues held their own separate championships until 1903, when they agreed to meet after the season in a playoff to determine an overall champion. The American League's Boston Americans defeated the Pittsburgh Pirates in that first "World Series," five games to three. Most baseball historians agree that the 1903 season was the start of baseball's "modern era." The rules of the sport had not changed dramatically from the previous years. But the familiar structure of a 154-game season (later expanded to 162 games in 1961), two individual league champions, and the World Series came into being and has remained so ever since.

debut with the Brooklyn Dodgers. In 1947, Robinson became the first African American to play in the majors in the modern era. At a time when only whites were permitted on big-league fields, Robinson's courage in the face of death threats and racial taunts helped break baseball's infamous "color barrier" and opened the door for black players. Robinson died in 1971. Baseball honored his legacy in 1997 by permanently retiring his number (42) and by issuing special patches with his uniform number for the players on all teams to wear on their sleeves. To this day, no major leaguer wears 42 on his back.

By contrast, the 1997 Dodgers are best remembered for two reasons: Piazza's monster season at the plate—arguably the best of all time for a catcher—and the team's lack of chemistry, which ultimately doomed Los Angeles's chances of reaching the postseason.

In late June, Piazza was in his usual spot—leading the team in batting average (.355). The Dodgers, meanwhile, were sleeping on the job. Their record at the end of the month was 39–42. A reporter from the *Los Angeles Times* asked Piazza for his opinion about the team's inconsistent play. As catcher, Piazza had his finger on the pulse of the team, and he freely spoke his mind: He pointed out that many of his teammates were from different countries and backgrounds, and lived in different neighborhoods, making it difficult to form friendships and build the trust needed to work together as a unit. Indeed, players would frequently brush right past one another in the Dodger clubhouse without saying a word. "You've got [Hideo] Nomo from Japan, Chan Ho [Park] from Korea," Piazza said. "You've got guys from the Dominican Republic and Mexico . . . so what do people expect? That all of a sudden we're going to be one big happy family? Of course not. Guys are going to have their groups that they're going to hang out with." Piazza was not laying the blame on any player in particular. He was simply expressing a fact—and trying to shake the team out of its funk. Still, saying

Mike Piazza ran down Kevin Orie of the Chicago Cubs, who was caught between home plate and third base, during a game on August 2, 1997, at Wrigley Field. Piazza was named National League Player of the Month in July and August of that year. In 1997, he hit .362 and belted 40 home runs.

out loud what everyone was thinking did not sit well with some teammates and fans, some of whom called him insensitive.

Piazza's bold statement seemed to do the trick—for a while. The Dodgers won 20 of 27 games in July and 19 of 30 in

August, and were on top of the National League West as late as September 17. They lost 12 of their last 19, though, finishing in second place and missing the playoffs with a final record of 88–74. Piazza, however, shined bigger and better than ever before. He won the National League's Player of the Month award two times, in July and August. On September 21, he launched a gargantuan home run at Dodger Stadium against the Colorado Rockies that carried over the left-field wall and completely out of the stadium. Only one player until then had managed that feat: Hall of Famer Willie Stargell. Piazza's .362 batting average was the highest by a catcher in 61 years and was third best in the majors that season. His 40 home runs set the single-season record for the Los Angeles Dodgers as did his 124 RBIs, and he was awarded his fifth-straight Silver Slugger trophy. The MVP award, however, went to Larry Walker of the Colorado Rockies, who batted .366, with 49 homers and 130 RBIs. Piazza finished second in the voting for the second year in a row.

Heading into 1998, Piazza was in a unique position. His value was at an all-time high, and he had one year left on his contract. He did not want to wait until the end of the next season to begin working out his next contract when his value might not be as high. So he decided to take advantage of his standing as the best hitting catcher in baseball and ask the Dodgers to offer him a new contract with a big raise. A very big raise: $13 million to $15 million per season for the next seven or eight years. Piazza really wanted to play his entire career with the Dodgers. The new contract would most likely give him that opportunity, he thought, and spare him the headache of having to negotiate two or three contracts down the road. Piazza gave the Dodger organization a deadline of February 15 to make a decision. Otherwise he would sell his services to other teams as a free agent at the end of the 1998 season.

Piazza's demand seemed greedy. In reality, it was just business. Owners make millions of dollars from ticket sales to fans who pay to see stars in action. Stars, in turn, help their teams succeed and reach the playoffs, during which the owners sell more tickets. It is only right that the stars should get a piece of the profits they help create. Piazza knew it was his time to cash in, and he also knew his demand was a test of the Dodgers' new ownership. Late in the 1997 season, Australian businessman Rupert Murdoch, the chairman and chief executive of News Corporation, the parent company of the Fox television network, announced that he was buying the Dodgers (the official purchase was finalized on March 15, 1998). Dodger fans and sports journalists were curious to see how Murdoch would react to Piazza's test and how willing Murdoch would be to spend the big bucks to sign free agents and improve the team.

In fact, Murdoch was ready to open his wallet. Just not at the price Piazza was asking. Piazza had no way of knowing that the rest of his baseball career would change because of that decision.

8

Starting Over

On May 15, 1998, the Dodgers rocked the sports world with an announcement few sports fans saw coming: Mike Piazza had been traded. As it turned out, Rupert Murdoch did not think he could sign Piazza to a contract that would make him happy. Rather than risk losing their All-Star catcher as a free agent at the end of the season, the Dodgers decided to send him to the Florida Marlins for as many big-name players as they could get. *Sports Illustrated* ranked the deal as the biggest trade in baseball history. Piazza, along with third baseman Todd Zeile, was shipped to Florida in exchange for five players. Among them were third baseman Bobby Bonilla, outfielder Gary Sheffield, and catcher Charles Johnson. All told, the seven players involved in the deal had 15 All-Star appearances among them, four 30-home run seasons, and $108.1 million worth of contracts.

The trade caught Piazza completely by surprise. Just one day before, the dashing Los Angeles sports idol had starred in a commercial filmed at Dodger Stadium for a new TV sports network. He got the news of his trade from the Dodgers' management that evening, as he was changing in the clubhouse after a game against the Phillies. Piazza staggered out of the stadium in shock and immediately called his agent, Dan Lozano, to tell him the news. As soon as the story broke to the public, sports call-in shows in Los Angeles were abuzz with outrage as fans could not believe the mistake their team had made. "You don't trade a Hall of Famer!" they cried.

It was just business. Piazza called his dad the next day to talk it over and then returned to Dodger Stadium in the evening. He began to pack up his locker before the game against the Montreal Expos. Tommy Lasorda arrived to give him a good-bye kiss on the cheek. Hideo Nomo, who had become a friend, asked him to autograph a jersey. Other players hugged him. Stadium workers asked him to pose for one last picture. As Piazza walked out of his home away from home as a Dodger for the last time, fans in the left-field seats caught sight of him near the players' parking lot and began to cheer for him. Piazza never looked up. He raised his right hand in brief thanks, a gesture grander than any he usually made on the field, where he preferred to let his hitting do the talking, just like his hero, Mike Schmidt. Then he hopped into his big red Cadillac and turned the radio on to listen to the game. Before long, he snapped it off and popped in a tape of some of his favorite music.

Piazza was smarting inside. "I'll remember the standing ovations, the people, the autographs. It's the end of a marriage," he told a *Sports Illustrated* reporter riding along with him. "That's sad. But it's not a death. Leaves fall off the trees. They grow back."

In fact, Piazza knew another big change was in the air. The Marlins had been trading away their highest-paid players after winning the World Series the previous fall. They wanted to save money and start building again with younger, cheaper talent. Piazza figured he would be a Marlin for only a short while until Florida could find another team that could offer him a big paycheck. He looked on the bright side in the meantime, thinking about the house he owned in Boynton Beach, Florida, near Miami, where the Marlins played their home games: "At least I can stay in my crib," he told the reporter.

WELCOME TO NEW YORK!

Piazza appeared in just five games for the Marlins when the word he had been waiting for came down on May 22: He was being traded to the New York Mets. If the call-in shows in Los Angeles had been buzzing after the trade from the Dodgers, the airwaves in New York caught fire when the announcement was made. The savior of the Mets was coming to town!

For more than 50 years, New York City had had three major-league teams: the Yankees, the Giants, and the Brooklyn Dodgers. The Dodgers moved to Los Angeles after the 1957 season, and the Giants followed to San Francisco at the same time. Fans of the two teams were heartbroken but drew some comfort when the Mets were born in 1962. The team became an instant fan favorite—mostly for the comical ways in which it would lose. The "lovable Mets," as they became known, lost a major-league record 120 games that first season. They stunned the baseball world, though, in 1969, by winning their first World Series. After that, the "Amazin' Mets" were usually hot or cold: They either finished in last place or near it, or they made it to the top. They were National League champions in 1973 (losing the World Series to the Oakland A's in seven games), and they won it all for the second time in 1986.

Piazza joined a Mets team that had scraped bottom in the early '90s (it lost 103 games in 1993) but was on the upswing. New York finished 1997 with 88 wins and 74 losses, its first winning season since 1990. On the day Piazza was traded, the

In his first game as a New York Met, Mike Piazza connected on an RBI double in the sixth inning against the Milwaukee Brewers on May 23, 1998. Eight days earlier, he had been traded from the Los Angeles Dodgers to the Florida Marlins. The Marlins dealt him to New York on May 22.

team's record was 24–20. The new addition to the team helped bump that up to 25–20 in his first game in a Mets uniform, on May 23. Piazza contributed a sixth-inning double and an RBI in a 3-0 win over the Milwaukee Brewers—and he received a standing ovation from the Shea Stadium crowd. "I'm on cloud nine right now," he said afterward to the *New York Times*. "But I need some sleep."

Actually, the Mets had not made the trade just for Piazza's bat. They hoped his star power would make the team glamorous and more fun to watch. The Mets were treated almost like a pesky little brother by the New York newspapers and radio and TV stations. Most of the headlines went to the Yankees, with their superstar Derek Jeter, their legends, including Babe Ruth and Mickey Mantle, and their tradition of winning World Series championships, the most recent in 1996. The Yankees' principal owner, George Steinbrenner, also generated mountains of publicity with his free-spending ways and his tantrums whenever his team lost. Piazza's arrival was a signal by the Mets' co-owners, Fred Wilpon and Nelson Doubleday, that they wanted to be taken seriously on the grand stage of New York sports, that they were willing to pay big bucks for free agents, and that they planned to win.

The Mets reeled off six more victories with Piazza behind the plate, giving New York a season-high nine-game winning streak. But Piazza fell into a power slump, perhaps dazed by the sudden changes in his life and the sky-high expectations of team management. He knocked in only eight runs in June and 14 in July, and the team lost 30 of 55 games. The Mets' fans felt cheated and blamed Piazza for the team's woes. They booed him whenever he made an out. They were also unhappy that he had taken the place of injured catcher Todd Hundley, one of their favorites.

In truth, Piazza was pressing at the plate. The Mets' general manager, Steve Phillips, had been talking with Dan Lozano about a new contract for the 29-year-old slugger, and Piazza was trying hard—perhaps too hard—to prove that he deserved the big raise he had originally sought from the Dodgers. "Last year was a career year for me, where everything went right, and it's tough to measure up to that," he told the *New York Daily News* on July 21. Finally, in late July, Phillips told Lozano that the team would wait until the end of the season to talk about the contract.

★ ★ ★ ★ ★ ★

SO, YOU WANT TO BE A GENERAL MANAGER?

The general manager, or GM, is the architect of a baseball team. His job is to build a winning roster of players through trades, free-agent signings, and the development of minor leaguers. He must be a shrewd judge of talent, keep his eye on the future, and have the guts to make tough decisions. That sometimes means he has to cut or trade a popular veteran to make room for a younger, unproven player with potential. At the same time, he must be ready to make a deal that will improve his lineup right away, usually to make a run at the playoffs. In that case, he may trade minor-league prospects for a proven veteran with postseason experience. Other duties of the GM include negotiating contracts and the hiring and firing of the manager and coaches.

At one time, most general managers were retired ballplayers or family members of the team owner. Today's GMs are a new breed. Many are young, have never played professionally, and have college degrees. They are also less likely to rely on old theories about what makes a good player. Instead, they pack a laptop full of charts and statistics that show the strengths of players in a variety of game situations, such as hitting with runners in scoring position.

One of the most influential general managers of the past few years is Theo Epstein of the Boston Red Sox. He became the youngest GM in the game's history when Boston hired him in November 2002 at age 28. The Yale University graduate showed he had brains by making a number of smart roster moves before the 2004 season. When the Sox slumped at midseason, he showed he had guts by trading popular shortstop Nomar Garciaparra for two key players. The gamble paid off when the Red Sox went on to win their first World Series championship in 86 years that fall.

The decision helped clear Piazza's mind and allowed him to concentrate on the game. Around the same time, the fans began to back off, realizing they might be chasing one of the sport's top hitters out of town. Bam! Piazza lit up. He hit .347 with 8 homers and 30 RBIs in August, and .378 with 6 homers and 22 RBIs in September. Behind his offense, the Mets went on a playoff push for the wild-card spot. They fell short by one game when they were swept by the Atlanta Braves in their final series of the season, and finished at 88–74. Still, the excitement of coming so close to making the playoffs for the first time since 1988 made everyone giddy. Piazza batted .328 on the season, fourth in the National League. He hit 32 home runs, including a league-best four grand slams, and he slugged his 200th career home run on September 21. At the end of the season, his sixth Silver Slugger trophy awaited him—and so did a new contract from the Mets.

Piazza signed for seven years at $91 million on October 26. His star power was worth the investment: In the 24 home games before he came to New York, the Mets drew an average of 18,112 fans per game. With Piazza in the lineup, the average was 34,589. "I knew New York was where I was meant to be," Piazza confessed to the *New York Daily News* at the press conference announcing his signing. "Mets fans deserve a championship. I want to be on that championship team."

Piazza's signing put a cap on a remarkable year in baseball. By most accounts, the sport rebounded from its low point following the strike settlement in 1995. More than 70.2 million fans went to the games, setting a new attendance record. Two exciting events helped drive the comeback: The Yankees steamrolled their opponents, setting a record for the most victories (114) in the regular season on their march to winning the World Series; and Mark McGwire of the St. Louis Cardinals and Sammy Sosa of the Chicago Cubs engaged in a dramatic summer-long chase of the home run record (61) for a single

After the 1998 season, Mike Piazza signed a seven-year, $91 million contract with the Mets. Here, he is pictured with the team's owners, Nelson Doubleday *(left)* and Fred Wilpon, at the news conference announcing the deal. By acquiring Piazza, with his star power, the Mets owners were hoping to add some luster to their team and to make the Mets a winner.

season. The two sluggers ended up rewriting the record books: McGwire hit 70 round-trippers, and Sosa finished with 66.

MAKING A NEW HOME

Piazza began to enjoy life as a New Yorker almost from the moment he arrived in the Big Apple. He rented a high-rise apartment in the city's fashionable Upper East Side neighborhood and bought a house in the nearby suburbs of New Jersey. He began to reach out to the community as well. In November, he visited a group of sick children at a hospital in New Hyde Park, New York. Piazza spent about 90 minutes with the kids, doing his best to cheer them up with jokes and horseplay. "I think it's important to reach out to people in general. I recognize that responsibility," Piazza told the *Daily News*. He also became involved in "Takin' It to the Fields," a Mets program that helps youth baseball leagues repair and improve their playing fields. Piazza donated more than $100,000 to the program from 1998 to 2001.

It was obvious whenever Piazza went out in public that the city was eager to embrace him as well, especially Mets fans. Unlike Yankees fans, who were used to a winner, the Mets faithful typically had low expectations. As Piazza strolled the streets of Manhattan, people called out to him. They saw him as a symbol of hope for a new era. "The support of this team is unprecedented," Piazza said in the *Daily News* interview. "It's blue-collar support. The people live and die with the team."

Why shouldn't the fans hope? The Mets had a legitimate shot at reaching the playoffs based on their 1998 success and the off-season moves being made by Phillips. In December, he traded away Todd Hundley in part to help keep Hundley's fans off Piazza's back. He added 40-year-old pitcher Orel Hershiser, Piazza's former Dodger teammate. Pitcher Al Leiter had been traded to the Mets in February 1998 after helping the Marlins win the World Series, and he was the ace of the staff. Phillips signed him to a new contract. The best leadoff hitter of all time, Rickey Henderson (66 steals in 1998), came on board as did free agent Robin Ventura, a slick-fielding, solid-hitting third baseman.

The plan for the Mets went like this: Compete with the mighty Atlanta Braves for first place in the National League East, go deep into the playoffs, and knock the Yankees out of the headlines. It was a tall order, and Piazza did his part. He batted .303 in 1999 and hit 40 home runs, making him the only catcher with two 40-homer seasons in a career. His 124 RBIs were third best in the National League and set a Mets record. He had a 24-game hitting streak in June, appeared in his seventh All-Star Game in July, and won his seventh Silver Slugger award.

In the end, the season did not work out exactly the way Phillips had planned, but it came close. The Mets were just one game behind the Braves on September 21, when the two teams began a three-game series in Atlanta. The Braves swept the Mets, triggering a seven-game losing streak for New York. The Amazin's wound up in a tie with the Cincinnati Reds for the wild-card spot and then beat the Reds in a one-game playoff to advance to the Division Series, in which they defeated the Arizona Diamondbacks, three games to one. That set up a showdown with the Braves in the National League Championship Series. The best-of-seven series was an absolute thriller, with the final five games each decided by one run. Game 5 was one for the ages: The Mets came back to win in the bottom of the fifteenth inning in the rain on a grand slam by Robin Ventura. In Game 6, the Mets staged two comebacks, tying the score, 7-7, in the top of the seventh on Piazza's two-run homer off of John Smoltz. After going ahead twice, though, the Mets could not hold the lead. They lost the game—and the series, four games to two—in the bottom of the eleventh inning when pitcher Kenny Rogers issued a heart-breaking walk to Andruw Jones with the bases loaded. It was a bitter pill to swallow for the Mets and their fans.

Despite Piazza's home run, heroics were in short supply for the Mets' catcher during the championship series. He had just four hits in 24 times at bat, and he made a costly first-inning error in Game 3 when he fired the ball into center field while trying to catch the Braves' Bret Boone stealing second. The errant throw allowed Gerald Williams to scamper home from third, scoring the only run of the game. Piazza was just

Mike Piazza talked about his injured thumb during a news conference before Game 3 in the 1999 National League Division Series against the Arizona Diamondbacks. The Mets won that series, but the physical exhaustion of a long season as catcher hampered Piazza's performance in the National League Championship Series against the Braves. Atlanta won the series in six games.

not at his best physically: He was worn out from catching in 30 of New York's final 32 regular-season games. He had had more bumps, bruises, aches, and pains than a paramedic's Powerpoint presentation. He sprained his right knee in April, suffered a slight concussion in June, and injured his left thumb in October. In the first five games of the Atlanta showdown, he was hit twice with a bat on backswings and was in two bone-crunching collisions at home plate. With a deep forearm bruise and a swollen hand, he could barely lift his left arm by the time the series reached Game 6.

Piazza had long ago established a reputation for playing through pain. Now he was 31 years old, and the talk began again about moving him to another position to keep his body in one piece and his bat in the lineup. As the Mets looked forward to a possible rematch with the Braves in 2000, Piazza also endured some picky questions from reporters about his leadership style. They wanted to know why Piazza, as the team's top slugger and superstar, did not try to fire up the Mets with rousing speeches in the clubhouse or fist-pumping displays on the field. Even some of his teammates quietly questioned why Piazza seemed to display so little emotion. Some thought he might be more concerned with his statistics and image than in helping the team. The criticism stung, and it was unfair. Piazza was simply old-school cool. "I definitely believe I'm a leader. But I believe I lead by example," he told the *New York Times* in April 1999. Steve Phillips leaped to his prized player's defense in the same article: "Mike doesn't have to be anything more than what he's always been. He doesn't have to be a vocal leader. He just has to go out and play like he's played—and do it for the next seven years."

9

The New York Years

Mike Piazza was like a zombie after the Atlanta series. "Losing was very devastating to him," his father told the *New York Daily News*. "It was so sad to see it lost that way . . . a grand slam, a base hit, anything other than to walk in the winning run. I know Mike felt destroyed." Worn out physically and emotionally, Piazza hung at home in October and "did absolutely nothing for three weeks," he told *Sports Illustrated* in August 2000. He slept and received massages to restore his beaten body; on Sundays, he spent all day in bed watching NFL games. After recovering, Piazza got back into fun. He took his new girlfriend, Darlene Bernaola, out to the clubs and restaurants that make New York one of the most glamorous cities in the world. The handsome sports star and the stunning California model were a photographer's dream, and they drew attention in the gossip columns. In February, Piazza appeared on the game show *Jeopardy* with two TV celebrities: actor Kevin Sorbo, the star of *Hercules*, and actress Jane Krakowski, from the nighttime comedy *Ally McBeal*. Piazza stepped up to the plate and defeated both, earning $15,000 for his teammate Al Leiter's charity.

Meanwhile, back at Shea Stadium, General Manager Steve Phillips was busy. He overhauled the New York roster by trading or releasing seven players. He beefed up the pitching staff by signing left-hander Mike Hampton, a free-agent star from the Houston Astros, and left-hander Bobby Jones from the Colorado Rockies. With the addition of Piazza's former Dodger (and Marlin) teammate Todd Zeile, Phillips hoped the retooled lineup would propel the near-miss team of the previous season to the next step: the World Series. In his wildest dream, Phillips could see the Mets beating Atlanta and then knocking off the Yankees in October to become the new kings of New York.

If Phillips had owned a crystal ball, he would have seen that his dream was not so wild. The Mets reached the World Series in 2000 in a season of thrills and chills like few before, with Piazza playing a central role in the drama. It all began 6,740 miles (10,847 kilometers) from Shea Stadium, in Tokyo, Japan, on March 29. In the first major-league game played outside of North America, the Mets and the Chicago Cubs met on Opening Day. The Cubs won, 5-3, with two of New York's runs coming on Piazza's eighth-inning home run, the first of 38 he would hit that season. On April 14, Piazza collected a career-high five hits in six turns at bat against the Pittsburgh Pirates, including a double and two home runs. The performance led to his eleventh career Player of the Week Award. In a June 30 game against the Braves, the Mets were trailing 8-1 in the bottom of the eighth when they scored a team-record 10 runs and came back to win, 11-8. Piazza's three-run homer was the deciding blow that put New York on top. The Mets would lead the majors with 45 come-from-behind victories in 2000.

Piazza was also at the center of one of the most talked-about incidents in baseball that year, on July 8. The Mets were playing an interleague game against the Yankees when rival pitcher Roger Clemens threw a 92-mile-per-hour (148-kilometer-per-hour) fastball that struck Piazza in the helmet. The star slugger crumpled to the dirt like a rag doll, and both teams rushed onto the field in an angry confrontation. After being helped to his feet, Piazza wobbled off the field and was later diagnosed with a concussion. The injury caused him to miss the All-Star Game three days later, though he had been the National League's No. 1 vote-getter. For days after the beaning, sportscasters, writers, and people on radio call-in shows debated whether Clemens had thrown at Piazza on purpose. Clemens said it was unintentional, but Piazza did not believe him. "He is a tremendously precise pitcher. He knows where the ball is going," Piazza told one writer. The skeptics certainly had a good case: The Yankees' ace had a reputation as an aggressive competitor who sometimes plunked batters he did not like—and he had plenty of reasons not to like Piazza. Before the beaning, the Mets catcher had 7 hits in 12 at-bats against Clemens, including 3 homers.

Piazza was back on his feet shortly after the All-Star Game and, by late August, the Mets were an unstoppable express train steaming toward the postseason. They won 16 of 19 games at one point and were only one loss behind the division-leading Braves. The Mets were 37–13 whenever Piazza drove in a run and 32–34 when he did not. Fully aware of Piazza's value now, and caught up in the excitement of winning, the Shea Stadium crowds chanted "MVP! MVP!" each time he stepped to the plate. New York finished the season with a record of 94–68, just one game behind Atlanta but comfortably in the wild-card spot. Piazza's .324 batting average tied him for tenth place in the National League, and his home-run total (38) was also tenth best. His RBI total (113) was just twelfth best, but another RBI stat was more telling: He averaged a run batted in every 4.3 times at bat. Only two other players averaged more RBIs that season. He earned his eighth Silver Slugger award and finished third in the MVP voting.

New York barreled through the first two rounds of the playoffs. They beat the San Francisco Giants in the Division Series, three games to one. Though Piazza's bat was cold (he hit just .214), the Mets pitchers did their part by shutting down the Giants' awesome slugger Barry Bonds, who batted just .176 with no homers. The National League Championship Series (NLCS) was next for New York, along with a possible rematch with the Braves. But a funny thing happened to the Braves on the way to the NLCS: They lost to the St. Louis Cardinals in the Division Series. Handed an early Christmas present, the Mets thanked the Cards by joyfully eliminating them in five games. This time, Piazza's bat was red hot: He hit safely in every game, batted .412, and socked two homers.

During the final game of the National League Championship Series, the Shea Stadium crowd could not contain its glee about reaching the World Series for the first time since 1986. They chanted, "We want the Yanks! We want the Yanks!" One day later, the Yankee Stadium crowd answered back, "We want the Mets! We want the Mets!" as the Yankees eliminated the Seattle Mariners in the American League Championship Series. With both New York teams in the World Series, Phillips's wild dream was one step closer to reality.

A SUBWAY SERIES

From 1947 to 1956, seven World Series were played entirely in New York between two of the city's three teams. Called a "subway series" because fans could travel by subway to each other's stadiums, the mighty Yankees appeared in all seven. They won five of six against the Dodgers and one against the Giants. It was a golden era of baseball in New York, and everybody was

Mets pitcher Mike Hampton and catcher Mike Piazza celebrated on October 16, 2000, after beating the St. Louis Cardinals in the National League Championship Series. Piazza hit safely in every game of the five-game series. The Mets would now face the New York Yankees in the first "subway series" in 44 years.

expected to declare his or her loyalty to a team—even if it meant brother against brother within the same household. "I was growing up in New York in the 1940s and '50s," Yankees manager Joe Torre told *Sports Illustrated* in October 2000. "The Yankees were always in the World Series, sometimes playing the Dodgers and sometimes the Giants. That was crazy. But a subway series now would be far wilder than that. . . . I have a feeling that this city is not going to be the same for the next 10 days."

Torre was right: The first all-New York World Series in 44 years electrified the city. Storeowners hung "Let's Go Mets!" signs in their windows. Delivery boys wore souvenir Yankee jerseys. Local newscasters declared their loyalties on TV, and the excitement spilled over to the players. Mets outfielder Benny Agbayani was just fooling around when he boasted on a radio show that his team would win the World Series in five games. The newspapers and TV stations reported it, and the joke grew bigger and bigger until it seemed like a real prediction. Some Yankees fans accused Agbayani of trash-talking. Piazza finally put a stop to the nonsense. "What do you want him to predict, that we're going to *lose* in five?" he said to a *New York Times* reporter on October 21.

Piazza was not looking for an answer, of course, but it seemed as if he had peered into Phillips's imaginary crystal ball. The Mets did, in fact, lose the World Series in five games—five emotional, nail-biting, fiercely fought games. Three were decided by one run, the other two by two runs. The Yankees took the opener, 4-3, in 12 innings in front of 55,913 crazies at Yankee Stadium. In Game 2, the Mets were down, 6-0, in the top of the ninth before staging a near comeback. They scored five runs in the inning—including two on a Piazza home run—before the Yankees finally escaped with a 6-5 victory. But that game may be best remembered more for a bizarre incident involving Piazza and Roger Clemens in their first showdown since the July 8 beaning. In the first inning, Clemens blazed

In the first inning of Game 2 of the 2000 World Series, Mike Piazza hit a foul ball that broke his bat into three pieces. Neither he nor Yankees pitcher Roger Clemens realized that the ball was foul. When the barrel of the bat landed near Clemens, he threw the broken piece toward Piazza, who was running to first base. "What's your problem?" Piazza shouted at Clemens. Earlier in the season, a Clemens fastball struck Piazza in the head, giving the catcher a concussion.

a fastball that shattered Piazza's bat into three pieces as he swung. The barrel of the bat bounced toward Clemens, and he fielded it instinctively like a baseball. Neither player seemed to realize that the ball had gone foul, and Piazza took off for first. The Yankee pitcher then threw the shattered piece toward Piazza, who stopped in his tracks when it landed near his feet. "What's your problem?" he shouted at Clemens. "What's your problem?"

Both teams rushed onto the field, but Clemens ignored Piazza and demanded a new baseball from the home-plate umpire. When tempers cooled and the game finally began again, Piazza grounded out to Clemens on the next pitch. The Yankee ace later said he did not mean to throw at Piazza, but like the summer incident, the skeptics had their case. Clemens was later fined $50,000 by Major League Baseball for his behavior.

The battle moved to Shea Stadium for the next three games. In Game 3, 55,299 fans went bonkers as the Mets broke a 2-2 tie in the bottom of the eighth and went on to win, 4-2. Game 4 went to the Yankees, 3-2, with both Mets runs coming on Piazza's third-inning home run. In Game 5, the Yankees scored twice in the top of the ninth to break a 2-2 tie and clinch the World Series with a 4-2 win. The game ended on Piazza's long fly ball to center field with a runner on second.

Once again, the labors of the long season and playoffs left Piazza's body and mind drained. He spent a few days at his parents' house in Pennsylvania and then drove south to his home in Boynton Beach, Florida, some 1,110 miles (1,786 kilometers) away. Piazza enjoyed taking long solitary drives. They helped him unwind and sort through his thoughts. "You really have a way of relating well to other people when you know yourself, spending time alone," he told the *New York Times*. Piazza's solo road trips had begun when he was a teenager working for his father in the summers. His job back then was to drive a truck loaded with used cars from dealerships to auto auctions across Pennsylvania and New Jersey.

On the long journey to Florida, Piazza pulled over whenever the spirit moved him—even at two in the morning to grab a snack. He listened to heavy metal or classical music. The hours alone gave him the opportunity to draw some conclusions about the events of the past nine months in a Mets uniform. The following March at spring training, he shared his thoughts with the *New York Times*: "The minute you start to feel so depressed, you kind of feel, 'Hey, we have a lot to be proud of,'" he told the reporter. "And the minute you say we have a lot to be proud of, you start to get depressed. You're in this sort of limbo." Piazza was expressing the frustration he felt over coming so close to reaching the mountaintop of success in Major League Baseball: a World Series championship. No doubt the thought crossed his mind that another long season was at hand, with all its bumps and bruises, ups and downs. Who knew if the Mets would make it back to the World Series, or if they would even reach the playoffs in 2001? Plenty could change between March and October.

SEPTEMBER 11

In fact, plenty did change—but in ways that had nothing to do with baseball. On the morning of September 11, Piazza was in his hotel room in Pittsburgh, Pennsylvania, sleeping in before the start of a three-game series with the Pirates. He was awakened by the phone ringing and ringing and ringing. His agent, Dan Lozano, was on the line. Lozano told Piazza to turn on the television. Like millions of other Americans, Piazza was stunned by the images on the screen.

Terrorists had attacked the United States. They hijacked four jet airliners and used them as weapons, crashing two into the World Trade Center towers in New York City and one into the Pentagon near Washington, D.C. The fourth crashed in a field in Shanksville, Pennsylvania. Almost 3,000 people lost their lives in the attacks. Most were killed when the two towers collapsed with victims trapped inside.

Mike Piazza wore the NYPD logo on his catcher's helmet during the Mets' game against the Atlanta Braves on September 21, 2001, at Shea Stadium. It was the first professional baseball game in New York after the 9/11 terrorist attacks. Piazza hit a two-run homer to lead the Mets to victory.

The Mets' games were postponed, and the team headed back home. They arrived in New York near midnight and were shocked at what they saw from the windows of their team bus: gray smoke rising in the sky from the burned remains of the towers, intense floodlights filling the area with white light as firefighters, police officers, and volunteers sorted through the charred, twisted metal looking for possible survivors. It was like a scene out of a horror movie.

☆ ☆ ☆ ☆ ☆

BASEBALL AFTER 9/11

The September 11 terrorist attacks on the World Trade Center in New York and the Pentagon near Washington, D.C., cast a dark light over the world of sports in 2001. Almost every pro and college sports event was canceled or postponed following the shocking assault. The NFL had begun its season just two days before. The league moved its Week 2 games to January, thus pushing back the Super Bowl by a week into February. In tennis, the American women's team withdrew from the Fed Cup tournament in Madrid, Spain. Golf's Ryder Cup matches in England were postponed until the following year.

Major League Baseball was enjoying a remarkable year when the attacks occurred. Barry Bonds had 63 home runs at the time, well on his way to setting a record of 73 on the year. Ichiro Suzuki, the Seattle Mariners' mysterious rookie from Japan, was intriguing fans with his quirky batting stance. He would go on to bat .350, best in the American League. After a week away, baseball picked back up again on September 17. Many teams staged patriotic tributes. They unfurled giant American flags across the

Before the start of the season, Piazza had moved to a new apartment in the city with a view of the towers from his balcony. Now, there was a hole in the skyline that tore at his heart. Baseball postponed all games for a week, and with their free time, Piazza and six teammates visited injured police officers, firefighters, and civilians in hospitals. "I have the feeling that I've been changed by all this," the catcher told *Sports Illustrated* on September 24. "We've all been changed. How

☆ ☆ ☆ ☆ ☆ ☆

diamonds at their stadiums in pregame ceremonies. Players wore American flag patches on their caps and sleeves. The mood among players and fans was somber and angry.

When the Yankees qualified for the World Series in October, it somehow seemed fitting that a New York team should get a chance to help soothe the spirit of the wounded city through sports. Games 1 and 2 were played in Phoenix, Arizona, home of the National League champion Diamondbacks. When the series returned to New York for Game 3, Yankee Stadium became the focus of the nation's emotional outpouring. Firefighters and police officers involved in the events of 9/11 were honored on the field. President George W. Bush threw out the ceremonial first pitch while a tattered flag pulled from the wreckage of the World Trade Center towers flew nearby. Players wore FDNY and NYPD caps.

In the end, Arizona won the World Series in a thrilling seven games. The last out was recorded in Phoenix on November 4. It remains the only time a World Series game has ever been played after October.

Ten-year-old Walter Matuza watched Mike Piazza demonstrate a catching technique during a baseball clinic in New York on January 22, 2002. The clinic was held for children who had lost parents during the terrorist attack on the World Trade Center.

can you not be?" Near Piazza's apartment, well-wishers placed flowers, candles, and sympathy cards at a firehouse that had lost 12 members in the towers. In all, 343 New York firefighters lost their lives.

The major-league season picked up again on September 17. The Mets went back to Pittsburgh, where they swept three games from the Pirates. Four days later, they played the Atlanta Braves at Shea Stadium in the first professional baseball game in New York since the attack. It was a powerful, stirring moment. Some of the Mets wore caps with FDNY on the front to honor the Fire Department of New York. Piazza's catcher's helmet had the NYPD logo of the New York Police Department. The rival teams hugged before the first pitch, and then, with the home team down, 2-1, in the eighth inning, Piazza put a theatrical ending on the heartfelt event: He smashed a two-run home run that clinched a Mets victory, 3-2. The 41,235 spectators at Shea Stadium shook the ground with a huge, tearful ovation.

The Mets played extremely well throughout September, winning 16 of 21 games. They were doomed, however, by a losing record in April, May, June, and October, and they finished out of the playoffs in third place behind the Philadelphia Phillies and the division champion Braves. Their final record: 82–80. Elsewhere in the majors, Barry Bonds hit 73 home runs to establish a new single-season record, and the Seattle Mariners won 116 regular-season games, breaking the mark set by the Yankees just three years before. In the World Series, the Arizona Diamondbacks defeated the Yankees on a come-from-behind, game-winning single in the bottom of the ninth in Game 7.

For the Mets' catcher, it was another typical Mike Piazza season. He hit his 300th career home run in July against the Phillies and was selected for his ninth-straight All-Star Game. He blasted his 306th career homer as a catcher on September 30, tying him with Yogi Berra for third all time among catchers. He batted .300, hit 36 home runs, drove in 94 RBIs, and found a place on a shelf for his ninth Silver Slugger trophy.

Like many New Yorkers, Piazza felt the need to help his city recover after September 11. He met a seven-year-old boy named Brendan whose father was a firefighter killed in action on that day. Brendan's dad had spoken about how much he admired Piazza for his hard work. Piazza spent time with Brendan at a local batting range, showing him how to hit. He invited the boy and his mother to his apartment to watch sports on TV, play video games, and talk. Piazza's generosity was simple, graceful, and came straight from his soul.

Piling Up
the Numbers

The 2002 season was a turning point for the Mets. General Manager Steve Phillips added some big-name veterans, including first baseman Mo Vaughn and second baseman Roberto Alomar, both former All-Stars. Phillips hoped their past glory would come alive and give the Mets' offense more pop. The strategy, though, was a disaster. Injuries and age took their toll. New York lost a National League-record 15 straight home games in August and September and skidded to a last-place record of 75 wins and 86 losses. It was the start of a downhill slide for the Mets that also resulted in losing records in 2003 and 2004.

Mike Piazza's 2002 season was also noteworthy. Now in his tenth major-league year, he continued to strike fear into the hearts of pitchers. He won his tenth Silver Slugger award.

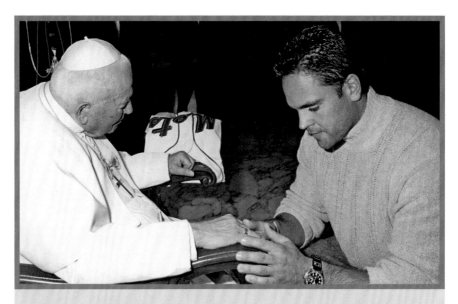

Mike Piazza knelt before Pope John Paul II on November 20, 2002, during the weekly general audience the pope held at the Vatican. Piazza, who presented the pope with a Mets jersey, was in Europe to promote Major League Baseball.

He batted .280, cracked 33 home runs, and added 98 RBIs. On August 17, he hit the 328th homer of his career as a catcher, giving him the all-time National League record. But 2002 would be Piazza's last full season at the top of his game. Over the next four seasons, injuries and the grind of catching would reduce his ability to perform at his best.

With his October free of the playoffs for the first time in three years, Piazza went on a three-week trip to Germany, France, and Italy to help promote Major League Baseball. He gave clinics on hitting and fielding to kids there. He also met with Pope John Paul II, the leader of the world's Catholic population. The experience was a deeply moving one for Piazza, who grew up Catholic and still attended Mass. He gave the Pope a souvenir Mets jersey and later described the visit as "humbling."

The following season, 2003, was perhaps the most frustrating of Piazza's career. Loss after loss weighed heavily on him, and he drove in just five runs in April, his lowest monthly total ever. In May, he suffered a groin injury and missed almost three months of play. True to his style, he homered in his first game back. He ended 2003 on an eight-game hitting streak. Appearing in just 68 games, he batted .286 with 11 home runs, and 34 RBIs.

In 2004, the great experiment everyone had talked about since Piazza's rookie season was finally put to the test: He was switched to another position. The Mets asked Piazza to alternate as a first baseman on days when he was not playing catcher. He started 68 games at first. (He was the catcher in 50 games and a designated hitter in eight.) The transition at age 35 proved too difficult, however, and Piazza looked awkward and out of place. He made eight errors. When critics sniped about his defense, backup catcher Vance Wilson jumped in to support Piazza: "First base is not an easy position," Wilson told the *New York Times* on July 22. "It's an adjustment, and there is a lot of respect for how Mike has taken on the challenge." The Mets and Piazza decided to end the experiment for good before the season was over.

The 2004 season did have its bright moments, however. On May 5, Piazza launched the first-inning home run against the San Francisco Giants that made him the all-time leader in homers by a catcher. The Mets honored Piazza's achievement six weeks later, on June 18. They invited four Hall of Fame catchers, Yogi Berra, Johnny Bench, Gary Carter, and Carlton Fisk—whose record of 351 homers Piazza had passed—to Shea Stadium for Mike Piazza Night. Fisk told MLB.com how much he and the other Hall of Famers admired Piazza's work ethic: "We, as catchers, can fully appreciate going behind the plate every day *and* putting [up] the numbers Mike has on the board," the 11-time All-Star said. Piazza's dad and Tommy Lasorda attended the pregame ceremony, during which the

Mets presented their hard-hitting backstop with the home plate he had crossed when he hit No. 352. Tears rolled down Mr. Piazza's face as the crowd of 36,141 cheered for his son. After all these years, Piazza and his dad remained close.

Another 2004 moment was more bizarre than bright, and once again it featured Piazza's nemesis, Roger Clemens. Piazza was chosen by baseball fans to be the National League's starting catcher at the All-Star Game, played on July 14. Clemens, now in the National League with the Houston Astros, was the starting pitcher. The hype about the two enemies working together as battery mates grew and grew. Both men claimed they had put their differences behind them, but doubts arose when Clemens gave up a surprising six runs in the first inning, the only inning he pitched. The media wondered: Had Piazza somehow tipped off American League batters about Clemens's pitches to get revenge? The idea was absurd but fun to debate. To his credit, Clemens tried to put a stop to the silly chatter in the postgame press conference by taking full responsibility for his poor performance.

Piazza finished the 2004 season with a .266 batting average, 20 home runs, and 54 RBIs. He was intentionally walked 14 times, tied for fourth in the league, a sign that pitchers still respected his powerful bat. He also had some fun off the field. In September, he appeared on an episode of *The Apprentice*, starring billionaire businessman Donald Trump. Piazza's role in the popular reality series was to help one of the contestants promote vanilla-flavored Crest toothpaste. He also had a chance to try out his rock 'n' roll chops at New York's Hard Rock Cafe in October, when he sang backup vocals with the heavy-metal band Overkill.

GOOD-BYE NEW YORK!

Piazza began 2005 with a happy change in his personal life. For the past few years, he had been dating Alicia Rickter, a 32-year-old former model from California who had appeared on

Mike Piazza and his wife, Alicia Rickter, a former model, posed for photographers in September 2005 at the grand opening of the new Hard Rock Cafe in Times Square in Manhattan. The two were married earlier in the year.

TV's *Baywatch*. Rickter had never been to a baseball game in her life when she first met Piazza, so the New York superstar introduced her to the sport by showing her a video of his home runs. "My motivation was to impress her," Piazza told *InStyle* magazine in 2005. It worked. On January 29, the couple married in a ceremony held at St. Jude Catholic Church in Miami. Piazza's brother Vincent served as best man, and guests included Mets teammates Al Leiter and John Franco. An elegant reception followed in a mansion on nearby Fisher Island. Upon returning to New York, the couple moved into a new apartment in the trendy TriBeCa neighborhood. Alicia resumed her studies at Manhattan Marymount College, where she was working toward a degree in psychology.

Back on the field, the Mets' three-year slide came to an end with a number of important roster changes in 2005. New general manager Omar Minaya signed free agent Pedro Martínez, one of the best pitchers of the previous decade. The former ace of the 2004 World Series champion Boston Red Sox instantly made the Mets a contender again. Martínez's star power also helped lure other top free agents to the team, including five-tool standout Carlos Beltrán. At the same time, the emergence of young, hungry players from the Mets' farm teams created electricity in the air at Shea Stadium and a focus on the future. Under rookie manager Willie Randolph, the Mets improved by 12 wins, finishing in third place with a record of 83–79.

Piazza's 2005 season was sentimental. He was in the last year of his seven-year contract, and he wanted to keep playing in 2006. He knew, though, that the chances were slim that the Mets would sign a 37-year-old catcher whose best days were behind him. On September 28, Mike was batting .256 with 18 home runs when he talked to the *New York Times* about what it was like to go from rookie phenom to aging veteran. "I compare it to a new car. When you get a new car, the power windows go up quick—it's quicker and you get

The Mets played a video of Mike Piazza highlights during the seventh-inning stretch of the final game of the 2005 season, on October 2. Here, Piazza acknowledges the fans during the tribute. The game would turn out to be Piazza's last one with the Mets.

more response. And then when it gets older, little things start to break. Things fall off. Our bodies are machines."

Now older and wiser, Piazza cared for his "machine" as if it were a shiny new Mercedes-Benz. His pregame meals included "some greens, carbs, and raw foods," he told *Stack* magazine. "These brain foods have really helped me out. . . . It sounds so basic and cliché, but a healthy diet, adequate rest, and taking care of your body are key."

On October 2, the Colorado Rockies were in town to play the Mets in the final game of the season at Shea Stadium. A video of Piazza's greatest moments in a Mets uniform began to play on the scoreboard during the seventh-inning stretch. The game stood still for eight minutes as 47,718 men, women, and children clapped along with the scenes to show their affection for the treasured superstar and all he had meant to New York. Players on both teams stood at the top of their dugouts and watched, too.

Piazza confessed later to the *New York Times* that he had nearly started to cry before the game. So many memories came back to him. "This was such a huge part of my life," he told the reporter. "It will always be a big part of my life, with the fans and the great times, and the tough times." Piazza grounded out to shortstop in his last at-bat. As he trotted off the diamond, the fans gave him a standing ovation. For once, the old-school cool catcher let the emotions wash over him on the field, and he blew kisses to the crowd.

HELLO SAN DIEGO!

Piazza batted .251 in 2005, with 19 home runs and 62 RBIs. Just as he suspected, the Mets did not offer him a new contract after the season. He soon found that very few teams were interested in his services. The Phillies talked with him about joining as a backup catcher. Piazza, though, believed that he was more effective as a starter and was not ready to be thought of as second string. The Yankees mentioned his name as a possible designated hitter, without making an offer. For the first time since the end of his college days, Piazza was at a crossroads in his baseball career.

Then the San Diego Padres came calling. The Padres needed veteran leadership behind the plate and a bat that packed some punch. Piazza fit the bill, and the two sides came up with a plan for him to serve as the starting catcher as often as he could with days off when he needed to rest his body. On other days he would be a designated hitter (when playing in interleague games) or a pinch hitter. The Padres signed Piazza to a one-year contract for $1.25 million, with the option of signing him for another year at $8 million at the end of the season. Describing the arrangement as a "natural fit," Piazza told reporters at a February 7 press conference, "At this time of my career, I know I need to pace myself so I can be the most effective. . . . As a player, you constantly have to try to reinvent yourself at times and adapt to what your role is."

Piazza looked forward to reporting for spring training at the Padres' camp in Peoria, Arizona. But first, he took a detour to Lakeland, Florida, to begin training for the World Baseball Classic, a new, 17-day international tournament made up of major leaguers and elite players representing their home countries. Piazza's Italian heritage gave him the opportunity to suit up for Italy—and promote the sport of baseball to the world as he had four years earlier in Europe. In his first game representing his grandparents' homeland, Piazza's double helped Team Italy defeat Australia, 10-0. Then, losses to Venezuela and the powerful Dominican Republic team led by David Ortiz and Albert Pujols knocked Piazza's team out of the tournament. Japan won the championship on March 20.

In a Padres uniform, Piazza had his best season since 2002 and played a pivotal role in San Diego's drive to a second straight National League West title. He appeared in 126 games and batted .283, with 68 RBIs. He hit 22 home runs, the most ever by a Padres catcher, and the second-most overall among

National League backstops in 2006. He collected his 2,000th career hit on July 21. Piazza's leadership behind the plate was also important to the team's success: In the 99 games in which he was the catcher, Padres pitchers had the lowest ERA (3.50) in the league.

A highlight of the season occurred when he returned to Shea Stadium for the first time as a Padre on August 8. The hometown fans gave their beloved ex-catcher a thunderous ovation when his name was announced. Piazza had one hit in four trips to the plate in his first game of the series. The next night, the crowd of 49,979 stood and cheered for about a minute as he dug into the batter's box. Piazza responded by tipping his helmet twice. By the end of the game, however, boos replaced the cheers—Piazza's two home runs had nearly stolen the victory away from the home team.

Unfortunately, the Padres' bats turned into toothpicks in the postseason. They produced just two hits in 32 chances with runners in scoring position against the St. Louis Cardinals in the National League Division Series. Unable to drive in runs effectively, San Diego was eliminated three games to one. (The Cardinals went on to win the World Series.)

After the series, San Diego general manager Kevin Towers reviewed his roster and made some changes. One involved Piazza. Looking to save money and build toward the future, Towers did not sign the 38-year-old catcher to a second season and let him go as a free agent. It was just business. Towers told ESPN.com: "[Mike] did a great job for us. . . . He's a tremendous guy in the clubhouse, a great leader. He proved that he's still got a lot left. He caught more ballgames than people expected."

The door was not closed on Piazza, however, after 14 seasons in a major-league uniform. In December 2006, he signed an $8.5 million, one-year contract with the Oakland Athletics. Set to play in the American League for the first time in his career, Piazza became the Athletics' new designated hitter. As the team's No. 3 catcher, he will occasionally help out behind the plate. "Swinging the bat, I'll do what I do: be a complete hitter and be a veteran in the lineup," he said on ESPN.com.

Piazza also added another star to his personal life two months later. On February 3, 2007, he became a first-time father when his wife, Alicia, gave birth to their daughter, Nicoletta Veronica. "You could tell he was ecstatic," his agent Dan Lozano said after Piazza told him the good news.

HALL OF FAME NUMBERS

Being elected to the Baseball Hall of Fame is the highest honor a major leaguer can hope for in his sport. It is a mark of excellence—a statement to the world that the player was one of the

☆ ☆ ☆ ☆ ☆ ☆
HALL OF FAME CATCHERS

From Buck Ewing to Gary Carter, the careers of the 13 Hall of Fame catchers cut across the history of the major leagues. Ewing is considered the greatest catcher of the nineteenth century. His days behind the plate began in 1880 with the Troy (New York) Trojans.

Back then, a catcher's gear was crude and offered very little protection. Like other players at the position, Ewing probably stuffed newspapers into his jersey to provide padding since the chest protector had not come into full use. In 1883, Ewing became the first catcher to hit 10 home runs in a season. He retired after the 1897 season and was inducted into the Hall of Fame in 1939. Gary Carter is the most recent inductee (2003). "The Kid," as he was called for his enthusiasm and joy, played from 1974 to 1992 for four teams. In 1986, he helped the New York Mets win the World Series. Here's a comparison of all 13 Hall of Fame catchers from the major leagues and the years in which they were inducted.

best of all time. To become eligible for the Hall, a player must have at least 10 years of major-league service and must be retired for five years. Each year, the Baseball Writers' Association of America reviews a list of 25 to 40 eligible candidates and its members cast their votes. The writers may vote for up to 10 candidates—the ones who receive 75 percent or more of all the ballots are elected into the Hall.

Of the thousands of players who have appeared in the major leagues, only 193 have received the highest honor. Just 13 of those are catchers. Entering the 2007 season, Piazza's lifetime stats fit right in with that elite group. His career batting average (.309) was better than all but two of the 13. He had

★ ★ ★ ★ ★ ★

Catcher	Year	BA	HR	RBI
Johnny Bench	1989	.267	389	1,376
Yogi Berra	1972	.285	358	1,430
Roger Bresnahan	1945	.279	26	530
Roy Campanella	1969	.276	242	856
Gary Carter	2003	.262	324	1,225
Mickey Cochrane	1947	.320	119	832
Bill Dickey	1954	.313	202	1,209
Buck Ewing	1939	.303	71	883
Rick Ferrell	1984	.281	28	734
Carlton Fisk	2000	.269	376	1,330
Gabby Hartnett	1955	.297	236	1,179
Ernie Lombardi	1986	.306	190	990
Ray Schalk	1955	.253	11	594

Year = Year Inducted; BA = Batting Average;
HR = Home Runs; RBI = Runs Batted In

more RBIs (1,291) than all but three. His slugging percent-age (.551), a measure of a hitter's power, was the best, and his home-run total (399) was also first. (Piazza's career total of 419 homers included those he hit while serving as a pinch hitter, a designated hitter, or a first baseman.)

But one other stat really sets Piazza apart from the group and says a lot about his bat control: He had never struck out more than 100 times in a season. That is a rare accomplish-ment for a power hitter. Only six other major leaguers with 400 career home runs and a lifetime batting average of .300 have accomplished that feat. None are catchers, and all are in the Hall of Fame: Babe Ruth, Lou Gehrig, Mel Ott, Ted Williams, Stan Musial, and Hank Aaron. Any player whose name can be included among that legendary group has the right to be proud—and can probably plan on a Hall of Fame induction ceremony.

Piazza has not revealed any concrete plans for his life once his baseball career is over. He has talked about taking a year off to think about what he wants to do next. "I'm going to enjoy doing a lot of nothing," he told MLB.com in May 2006. One thought is to go into broadcasting. Another is to spend more time on the golf course. (He and his father own the Bellewood Golf Club in Pennsylvania.) Whatever Piazza does, you know he will give it the same passion and energy he has given his major-league career—a career he hopes others will look back on not just for the hits, the home runs, and the awards, but also for the inspiring qualities that enabled him to succeed.

"I just want to be remembered as a guy who didn't have a lot of physical ability, but was determined," he told *Stack* maga-zine. "[A guy who] worked hard and didn't let anyone tell him he couldn't do it; and then, when he got to the top level, he played hard every day and made the most of his ability."

STATISTICS

MIKE PIAZZA

Primary position: Catcher (also 1B; DH)

Full name: Michael Joseph Piazza • Born: September 4, 1968, Norristown, Pennsylvania • Height: 6'3" • Weight: 215 lbs. • Teams: Los Angeles Dodgers (1992–1998); Florida Marlins (1998); New York Mets (1998–2005); San Diego Padres (2006); Oakland Athletics (2007)

YEAR	TEAM	G	AB	H	HR	RBI	BA
1992	LAD	21	69	16	1	7	.232
1993	LAD	149	547	174	35	112	.318
1994	LAD	107	405	129	24	92	.319
1995	LAD	112	434	150	32	93	.346
1996	LAD	148	547	184	36	105	.336
1997	LAD	152	556	201	40	124	.362
1998	LAD/FLA/NYM	151	561	184	32	111	.328
1999	NYM	141	534	162	40	124	.303
2000	NYM	136	482	156	38	113	.324
2001	NYM	141	503	151	36	94	.300
2002	NYM	135	478	134	33	98	.280
2003	NYM	68	234	67	11	34	.286
2004	NYM	129	455	121	20	54	.266
2005	NYM	113	398	100	19	62	.251
2006	SDP	126	399	113	22	68	.283
TOTALS		1,829	6,602	2,042	419	1,291	.309

Key: LAD = Los Angeles Dodgers; FLA = Florida Marlins; NYM = New York Mets; SDP = San Diego Padres; G = Games; AB = At-bats; H = Hits; HR = Home runs; RBI = Runs batted in; BA = Batting average

CHRONOLOGY

1968   September 4 Is born in Norristown, Pennsylvania.

1984   Receives batting tips at the age of 16 from Hall of Fame outfielder Ted Williams.

1988   June Is drafted in the sixty-second round by the Los Angeles Dodgers.

1989   June Begins his professional career by joining the Dodgers' minor-league team in Salem, Oregon.

1991   Hits 29 home runs while playing for the Dodgers' minor-league team in Bakersfield, California, the most of any player in the Dodgers' farm system that season.

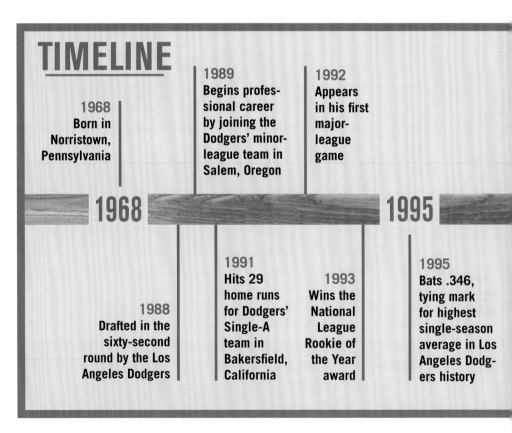

TIMELINE

1968
Born in Norristown, Pennsylvania

1989
Begins professional career by joining the Dodgers' minor-league team in Salem, Oregon

1992
Appears in his first major-league game

1968

1995

1988
Drafted in the sixty-second round by the Los Angeles Dodgers

1991
Hits 29 home runs for Dodgers' Single-A team in Bakersfield, California

1993
Wins the National League Rookie of the Year award

1995
Bats .346, tying mark for highest single-season average in Los Angeles Dodgers history

1992   **September 1** Appears in his first major-league game; collects three hits in three turns at bat versus the Chicago Cubs.

September 12 Slugs his first major-league home run in a game against the San Francisco Giants.

1993   Wins the National League Rookie of the Year award.

1995   Bats .346, tying Tommy Davis for the highest single-season average in Los Angeles Dodgers history.

1996   **July 9** Wins the Most Valuable Player award at the All-Star Game; drives in two runs with a homer and a double.

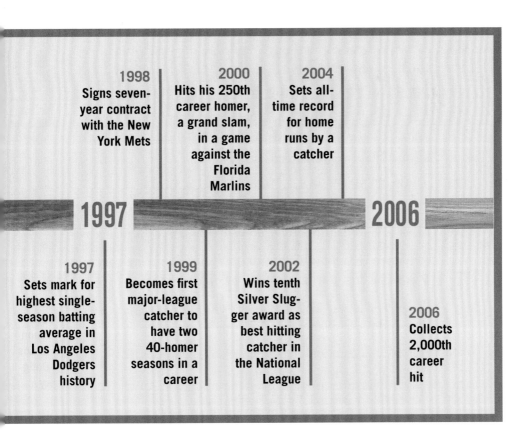

1998
Signs seven-year contract with the New York Mets

2000
Hits his 250th career homer, a grand slam, in a game against the Florida Marlins

2004
Sets all-time record for home runs by a catcher

1997

2006

1997
Sets mark for highest single-season batting average in Los Angeles Dodgers history

1999
Becomes first major-league catcher to have two 40-homer seasons in a career

2002
Wins tenth Silver Slugger award as best hitting catcher in the National League

2006
Collects 2,000th career hit

1997   January 21 Reaches a two-year, $15 million deal
         with the Dodgers

         Bats .362, setting the mark for the highest
         single-season average in Los Angeles Dodgers history.

1998   May 14 Is traded from the Dodgers to the Florida
         Marlins in a seven-player deal; is traded again to
         the New York Mets a little more than a week later;
         signs a seven-year contract with the Mets worth
         $91 million.

2000   May 4 Hits his 250th career homer, a grand slam,
         in a game against the Florida Marlins.

         October Appears in the World Series for the first
         time; hits two home runs in a losing cause against
         the New York Yankees.

2002   Wins his tenth Silver Slugger award as the best hitting
         catcher in the National League; only outfielder Barry
         Bonds has won the award more often (12 times).

2004   May 5 Breaks Carlton Fisk's record for most home
         runs (351) by a catcher with a first-inning shot
         against the San Francisco Giants.

2005   January 29 Marries Alicia Rickter, a model from
         California.

2006   January 29 Joins the San Diego Padres as a free agent.

         July 21 Collects his 2,000th career hit in
         a game against the San Francisco Giants.

         December 8 Signs a one-year deal with the
         Oakland A's to be their new designated hitter.

2007   February 3 Becomes a first-time father when his wife,
         Alicia, gives birth to a daughter.

GLOSSARY

at-bat   An official turn at batting that is charged to a baseball player except when the player walks, sacrifices, is hit by a pitched ball, or is interfered with by a catcher. At-bats are used to calculate a player's batting average and slugging percentage.

backstop   A slang word for catcher.

batter's box   A rectangle on either side of home plate in which the batter must be standing for fair play to resume.

battery   The pitcher and catcher considered as a single unit.

batting average   A measure of how often a batter gets a hit each time he is at bat. Batting average is computed by dividing the number of hits by the number of at-bats. A player with an average of .300 or better is considered a very good hitter.

bottom of an inning   The second half of an inning, usually when the home team bats. An inning is complete when both teams have been at bat and made three outs each.

bunt   A ball not fully hit, with the batter either intending to get to first base before the infielder can field the ball or allowing an existing baserunner to advance a base.

designated hitter   A player who bats in place of the pitcher throughout the game. (The National League does not use the designated hitter.) Since pitchers are traditionally poor hitters, the designated hitter provides more offense for a team.

double play   A play by the defense during which two offensive players are put out in a continuous action.

earned-run average (ERA)   The average number of runs a pitcher allows per nine-inning game; the runs must be scored without errors by defensive players.

error   The game's scorer designates an error when a defensive player makes a mistake resulting in a runner reaching base.

farm team   A team that provides training and experience for young players, with the expectation that successful players will move to the major leagues.

fastball   A pitch that is thrown more for high velocity than for movement; it is the most common type of pitch.

five-tool player   A player who has excellent fielding skills, a good throwing arm, and the ability to steal bases and hit for both batting average and power.

foul ball   A batted ball that lands in foul territory, which is the part of the playing field that is outside the first- and third-base foul lines. The foul lines themselves are in fair territory.

free agent   A professional athlete who is free to negotiate a contract with any team.

games behind   A statistic used in team standings. It is figured by adding the difference in wins between a trailing team and the leader to the difference in losses, and dividing by two. So a team that is three games behind may trail by three in the win column and three in the loss column, or four and two, or any other combination of wins and losses totaling six.

grand slam   A home run struck with runners on every base.

intentional walk   A walk given by a pitcher, normally by throwing four straight balls well outside of the strike zone. Often an intentional walk occurs with first base open, since the walk does not dramatically benefit the offense and opens up a chance for a double play. An intentional walk is seen as a compliment to the batter being walked and as an insult to the batter on deck, who is thought to be an easy out.

labor agreement   A contract between an employer and its employees that spells out a number of rules, such as: how much the employees can be paid, how often they will be paid, the benefits they will receive, and working conditions.

Most Valuable Player (MVP)   An award given to one player in each league voted as the most valuable to his team's success during the regular season.

runs batted in (RBI)   A batter is credited with an RBI when he gets a hit that allows a runner on base to score a run. He can also receive credit if he draws a walk with the bases loaded, which forces a runner on third to come home.

slugging percentage   A measure of the power of a batter. Slugging percentage is calculated by dividing total bases of all the player's hits by the number of at-bats. (Total bases on a single = 1; a double = 2; a triple = 3; a home run = 4.)

strike zone   The area directly over home plate up to the batter's chest (roughly where the batter's uniform lettering is) and down to his knees.

top of an inning   The first half of an inning, usually when the away team bats. An inning is complete when both teams have been at bat and made three outs each.

BIBLIOGRAPHY

"All-Star Results—1996," MLB.com. Available online at *http://mlb.mlb.com*. Downloaded: August 12, 2006.

Antonen, Mel. "Piazza Works Hard on Fundamentals." *USA Today*, October 28, 1993.

Associated Press. "Dodgers' Piazza Is Hot." *San Francisco Chronicle*, June 23, 1993.

———. "Dodgers Win in 13th." *San Francisco Chronicle*, September 2, 1992.

Baer, Susan. "Major-League Romance." *InStyle*, Summer 2005.

Bamberger, Michael. "Playin' the Dodger Blues." *Sports Illustrated*, May 25, 1998 (Volume 88, Issue 21): pp. 32–40.

Beaton, Rod. "Reggie Smith a Hit With Dodgers." *USA Today*, May 23, 1994.

Cook, Kevin. "The Playboy Interview: Mike Piazza." *Playboy*, June 2003.

Crasnick, Jerry. "Minor League Memories: From Last to First," Attheyard.com. Available online at *www.attheyard.com/minorleaguememories/article_564.shtml*. August 1, 2004.

Diamos, Jason. "Piazza Embraces New York Challenge." *New York Times*, April 4, 1999.

———. "Piazza Swings a Bat and Suddenly It's the 80's." *New York Times*, May 24, 1998.

Friend, Tom. "An Era Concludes in the Dodgers' Dugout As Lasorda Steps Down After 2 Decades." *New York Times*, July 30, 1996.

Goodman, Michael J. "Pumped Up Dodger Catcher." *Los Angeles Times Magazine*, April 3, 1994.

Hale, Mark. "Oh, Baby! Piazza's a Dad." *New York Post*, February 6, 2007.

Hudson, Maryann. "Dodgers Get Out Erasers for 1993 Baseball." *Los Angeles Times*, April 5, 1993.

———. "Piazza Shies From Attention." *Los Angeles Times*, March 17, 1994.

———. "Piazza's Storybook Season Now Has a Perfect Ending." *Los Angeles Times*, October 28, 1993.

James, Brant. *Mike Piazza*. Philadelphia, Pa.: Chelsea House Publishers, 1997.

Jenkins, Lee. "Piazza's Mighty Swat Breaks Fisk's Mark." *New York Times*, May 6, 2004.

Kepner, Tyler. "One Is Not the Loneliest Number." *New York Times*, March 5, 2001.

Leinweaver, Mark. *Minor Moments, Major Memories: Baseball's Best Players Recall Life in the Minor Leagues*. Guilford, Conn.: The Lyons Press, 2005.

Marini, Victoria, ed. *Piazza: Daily News*. New York: Sports Publishing Inc., 2000.

Moore, David Leon. "Piazza Legend Builds on Power." *USA Today*, June 25, 1993.

"My Favorite Book," *Sports Illustrated for Kids*, September 2000.

Newhan, Ross. "Open Mike." *Los Angeles Times*, June 26, 1997.

Nightengale, Bob. "Dodger Pitchers to Piazza: Thank You, Masked Man." *Los Angeles Times*, September 19, 1996.

———. "Not Even Piazza Is Escaping Criticism." *Los Angeles Times*, August 27, 1995.

———. "Piazza's Big Catch: 2 Years, $15 Million." *Los Angeles Times*, January 22, 1997.

———. "Piazza Could Return to Lineup Friday." *Los Angeles Times*, May 30, 1996.

Noble, Marty. *Mike Piazza: Mike and the Mets.* New York: Sports Publishing Inc., 1999.

Plaschke, Bill. "Nothing Light About Piazza." *Los Angeles Times*, September 2, 1992.

Platt, Ben. "Wild Pitches With Mike Piazza," MLB.com. Available online at *http://mlb.mlb.com.* May 13, 2006.

Popper, Steve. "Piazza Goes to Bat for Valentine's Lineup Decision." *New York Times*, October 21, 2000.

Roberts, Selena. "Mets Learn There's No Place to Hide Piazza on Defense." *New York Times*, July 22, 2004.

Rolfe, John. "Catching the Beat." *Sports Illustrated for Kids*, June 1995.

Schwarz, Alan. "As Bodies Mull Retirement, 2 Aging Stars Play On." *New York Times*, September 28, 2005.

Seeley, Don. "The Piazzas Build a Strong Family Foundation." *Pottstown Mercury*, July 27, 2004.

Shpigel, Ben. "For Piazza and Mets' Fans, a Last Embrace Before Letting Go." *New York Times*, October 3, 2005.

———. "Piazza, With No Regrets, Is Eager to Make a Fresh Start." *New York Times*, February 7, 2006.

Singer, Tom. "One on One: Mike Piazza." *Sport*, May 1994 (Vol. 85, Issue 5): pp. 26–27.

Smith, Chris. "Are the Mets Cursed?" *New York*, October 2, 2000 (Vol. 33, No. 38): pp. 30–35.

Smith, Claire. "The All-Star Game: Piazza, Campanella and Lasorda." *New York Times*, July 12, 1993.

Staph, Josh. "The Life: Starring Mike Piazza," Stackmag.com. Available online at *http://www.stackmag.com/TheIssue/ArticleDraw/3488.* May 2006.

Verducci, Tom. "Catch This!" *Sports Illustrated*, August 21, 2000 (Vol. 93, No. 7): pp. 38–43.

———. "Near, Yet So Far: The View from Mike's Balcony Was Changed Forever." *Sports Illustrated*, September 24, 2001 (Vol. 95, No. 12): pp. 36–37.

———. "N.Y., N.Y." *Sports Illustrated*, October 23, 2000 (Vol. 93, No. 16): pp. 48–58.

———. "Roger & Out." *Sports Illustrated*, October 30, 2000 (Vol. 93, No. 17) pp. 40–45.

"We're History." *Sports Illustrated for Kids*, April 1998.

Whiteside, Kelly. "A Piazza With Everything." *Sports Illustrated*, July 5, 1993 (Vol. 79): pp. 12–17.

———. "Baseball Anonymous at Dodgertown." *Sports Illustrated*, March 13, 1995 (Vol. 82): pp. 28–31.

FURTHER READING

BOOKS

Louis, Nancy. *Ground Zero*. Edina, Minn.: ABDO Publishing Co., 2002.

Marini, Victoria, ed. *Piazza: Daily News*. New York: Sports Publishing Inc., 2000.

McNeil, William F. *Backstop: A History of the Catcher and a Sabermetric Ranking of 50 All-Time Greats*. Jefferson, N.C.: McFarland & Co., 2006.

Robinson, Sharon. *Promises to Keep: How Jackie Robinson Changed America*. New York: Scholastic Press, 2004.

The Visual Dictionary of Baseball. London, England: DK Children, 2001.

WEB SITES

Baseball Almanac
www.baseball-almanac.com/

Encyclopedia of Catchers
http://members.tripod.com/bb_catchers/catchers/list.htm

www.baseballcatchers.com

Little League Online
www.littleleague.org/

MLB.com
http://mlb.mlb.com/index.jsp

National Baseball Hall of Fame Museum
www.baseballhalloffame.org/

PERIODICALS

ESPN the magazine

Sports Illustrated

Sports Illustrated For Kids

PICTURE CREDITS

INDEX

ABOUT THE AUTHOR

NICK FRIEDMAN is a freelance writer who specializes in children's nonfiction. He is a former senior editor with *Sports Illustrated For Kids* magazine, where he produced numerous articles about amateur and professional athletes. He has also written about current events, science, math, and health issues for Scholastic Inc.